Elizabeth College

Design for Elizabeth College
Guernsey March 1826

A History of

ELIZABETH COLLEGE

GUERNSEY

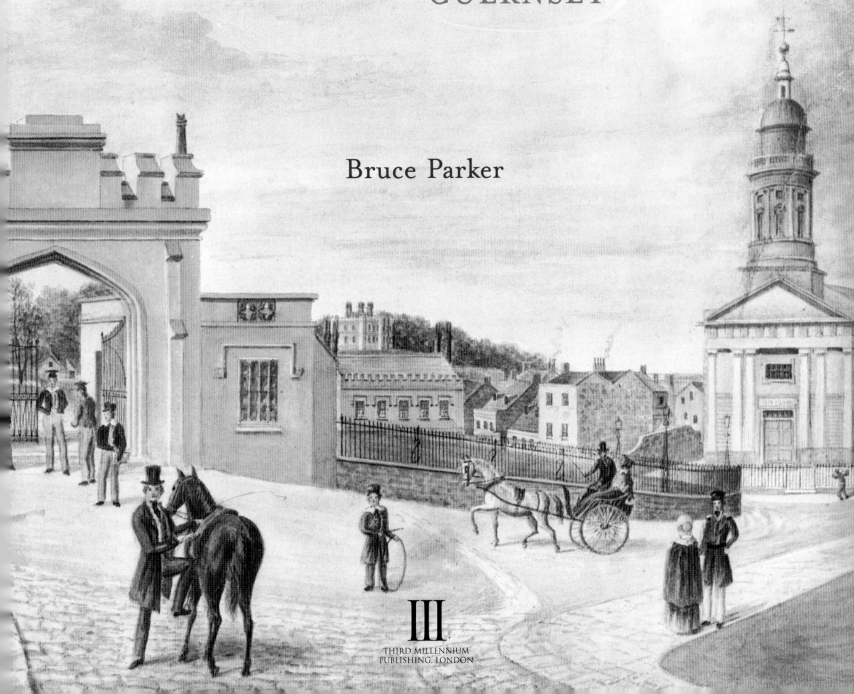

A History of
ELIZABETH COLLEGE
GUERNSEY

Bruce Parker

III

THIRD MILLENNIUM
PUBLISHING, LONDON

© Third Millennium Publishing Limited and
Elizabeth College

Bruce Parker has asserted his right to be identified as
the author of this work in accordance with the
Copyright, Designs and Patents Act 1988.

First published in 2011 by
Third Millennium Publishing Limited, a subsidiary
of Third Millennium Information Limited

2–5 Benjamin Street
London
United Kingdom
EC1M 5QL
www.tmiltd.com

ISBN 978 1 906507 50 3

British Library Cataloguing in Publication Data.
A CIP catalogue record for this book is available
from the British Library.

Project Manager: Susan Millership
Designer: Helen Swansbourne
Production: Bonnie Murray
Reprographics: Studio Fasoli, Italy
Printing: Gorenjski Tisk, Slovenia

Illustrations

Jacket front: View of St Peter Port taken by John Fitzgerald.

Endpapers: Architectural drawings of the east and west
elevations of Elizabeth College by John Wilson, 1825.

Title pages: *Elizabeth College, Guernsey*, 1843, by JH Matthiason.

CONTENTS

AUTHOR'S PREFACE

*W*RITING AND RESEARCHING this history of Elizabeth College has been a fascinating journey. My aim has been to tell the story, where possible, through archive correspondence, minutes of meetings and the observations of former Principals, masters and Old Elizabethans (OEs). It is not meant to be an academic work, but I hope it is accurate enough to appeal to historians while, at the same time, remaining readable by all who have an ordinary interest in this great school. I hope purists will forgive me when, in the interests of clarity, I have occasionally taken the liberty of changing some spellings in direct quotations.

I apologise to anyone who thinks any particular aspect of College life has not had a fair crack of the whip, or I have failed to give due recognition to a particular master or distinguished Old Elizabethan: the great difficulty I have faced has been deciding what to include and what to omit – this book could easily have been twice its size. As far as possible, I have kept away from lists of achievements by present-day Elizabethans and OEs – the five volumes of the Register do that admirably. Any errors are mine and mine alone. To non-OE readers, the figures which follow some names are the school numbers given to pupils when they arrive.

I cannot underestimate the help I have had from so many people but, particularly, Alan Cross, a much-loved former master and true servant of the College. He has translated Latin texts and his recollections have been a great source of information – at times, hugely amusing and deliciously indiscreet. Dr Darryl Ogier of the Guernsey Archives has answered the stupidest of my questions and kept me from straying into journalistic tendencies when I have found 'a good story'. I am truly grateful to him for his wisdom and freely given advice: the island is lucky to have him in charge of its archives.

Lastly, I have dedicated this book to three special women: Suzanne, my wife, who has put up with tales of Elizabethan discovery at every mealtime; Dot Carruthers, a never-failing source of good-humoured support, wisdom and encouragement, without whom this book would never have got off the ground, let alone been published; and Dot's office colleague, Sara Wright, who always knows what has to be done and then does it.

BRUCE PARKER

FOREWORD

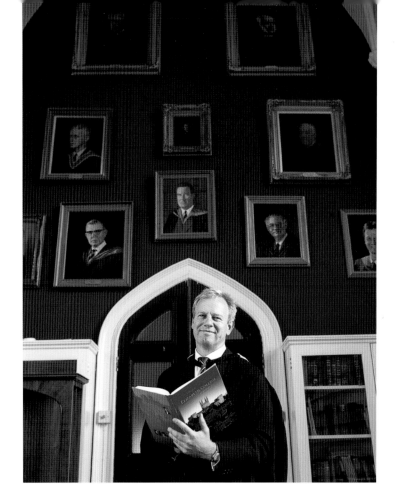

I AM DELIGHTED TO introduce this marvellous new complete history of Elizabeth College, brilliantly written by OE Bruce Parker. Bruce has produced a rollicking good read, which entertains from the very first pages with the College founded amid a potent cocktail of the Reformation, witchcraft and the great Sovereign herself. Thereafter, for a long while we hear of all manner of scandals, triumphs and shenanigans, before the calming influence of the College's re-chartering in 1824 and the construction of the striking skyline building we know so well today.

What becomes increasingly clear, however, is that Elizabeth College is far more than just a collection of buildings. We are introduced to a myriad of colourful pupils, teachers and headmasters who collectively serve to show what a remarkable school it is, and notably one of far and wide-reaching influence. In particular, one is constantly reminded of the school's seemingly ceaseless ability to produce outstanding young men (including four holders of the Victoria Cross) who are flung out to the four corners of the world to make their mark.

With this fine book being produced in time to celebrate Elizabeth College's 450th anniversary, I am pleased and extremely proud to report that we have a school today in particularly fine fettle. With over 750 pupils, record examination results and a busier-than-ever sporting and extra-curricular programme, one could certainly say that the College is firing on all cylinders. There are exciting times ahead, too: a much-needed refectory on top of the Old Gym will be followed by further development of facilities and educational opportunities to suit the demands of a top class, 21st-century education.

Any institution that survives for such a remarkable length of time must possess special and distinctive qualities. Themes of academic excellence, an emphasis on good character and notions of great service and leadership emerge clearly to remind us that this modest-sized island school has always punched far above its weight, and will continue to do so for many years to come: *Semper Eadem*!

GJ HARTLEY
Principal

SUBSCRIBERS

The Old Elizabethan Association would like to thank the following Subscribers
who have through their generosity funded the publication of this work:

Babbé, Guernsey Advocates

Carey Olsen

Cenkos Channel Islands

Rawlinson & Hunter Limited

Saffery Champness

Specsavers Optical Group Limited

Trust Corporation of the Channel Islands Limited

Nigel Allen (5512)
David E Allett (7428)
Anderson family (10634)
Will (7745), Archie (10597) &
    Alexa (10915) Annan
PJG Atkinson (5980)
Peter Bachmann (4755)
Max (10222) & Phineas (10635) Barber
Michael E Best (4508)
Michael Betley (7396) & family
Richard (5756) &
    Alexander (9641) Bird
William Bishop (9799)
Andrew P Bisson (4735)
Bryan Bisson (4980)
John R Bisson (4814)
Simon P Blondel (9459)
Nick Blows (9429)

Robin L Bougourd (5611)
Nick Brett (5586)
James Burge (5724)
Ray Bushell (6413)
Ben Byrom (8184)
Griff Caldwell (3873)
Adrian C Carey (6401)
Nigel Carey (5297)
Dot Carruthers & family
Daniel Carvill (9644)
Trevor Casbolt (6247)
Rob Champion (4388)
David Chan OBE (6883)
James Chan (10330)
Nicholas Chan (7565)
Jacob Cherry (10142)
Russell (7633) &
    Edward Clark (10707)

Matthew Colfer (10529)
R J Collas (5699)
Canon VJ Collas (4014)
Thelma Collenette neé Shaw
Oliver Connolly (10604) &
    Ian Le Noury (7888)
RJ Coppolo (8637)
Michael Creber (10030)
Sam Crosby (10269)
AMA Cross (7161)
Robert Cuerden (5120)
D Glyn Davies (4401)
John A Davis (4279)
Stephen T de Garis (4682)
Brian R & Glennys de Jersey
Steven (7754) & James (8001) de Jersey
Chris de Putron (7811)
Dips de Putron (4482)

Ben Dewsnip (9444)
Anthony L Dorey (4256)
Geoffrey Dorey (4992)
JHF Doulton
Peter Dumont (5820)
Neal M Duquemin (5999)
MJS Eades (6529)
SWS Eades (6530)
Adam East (6517)
Dr JA Elder (8265)
Alan Enevoldsen (5093)
Keith Enevoldsen (6173)
Finley (10701) & Max (10809) Evans
Stuart Falla MBE (5822)
Nick Ferris (7035)
Miles Finnerty (10461) and family
John Fitzgerald (6372)
Stephen Foote (7003)
Adrian Frampton (6272)
Charles Frossard (3929)
Terence Gale (4883)
Jonathan (7061), Andrew (9946) &
    Christian (10191) Gamble
Mike, Kate, George (10089) &
    Millie (10392) Garnett
Ian Gee (6596)
Jurat PST Girard (5442)
Major RL Goodison MBE (5374)
Godfray Guilbert (5304)
Jamie Hardie (10665)
Simon, Selena, Don (10194) &
    Hugo (10493) Harty
PA Harwood (5306)
Geoffrey Heggs (4151)
Mark Helyar (7170)
Tim Henderson (4762)
Matthew Henry (7544)
Barton Higgs (4093)
Matthew (9554), Barney (9743),
    Ollie (10092) & Amelia (10495)
    Hudson
Gary A Hunt (6890)
Callum Hunter (10496)
Edward (10763), Lucas (10764) &
    Josephine Hjorth Jeffreys
Jamie Jenner (10286)
Peter Johnston (4830)
Richard Kirkpatrick (4865)
BR Le Huray (8699)
Sir Peter Le Cheminant (3946)

RJ Le Feuvre (4367)
Stuart (6178), Jane, Matthew (9860),
    Alexander (10200) & James (10199)
    Le Maitre
Ben (10129) & Henry (10546) Le Page
Joe Le Page (9386)
Mark W (7015), James MP (9927) &
    Fraser W (10547) Le Tissier
Lynn Lewis (4467)
Alex Lindsay (5618)
Dr Bruce Lloyd (4768)
The late Ian (4858) & Sue Lloyd
Tim Lomax (7624) & George
    Cunningham Lomax (10980)
L Justin Malcic (10669)
Charles N Mallett (4230)
John Mann (5262)
Michael Marshall (4172)
Derek Martel (4636)
Norman Martel (5098)
Peter J Martel (4497)
Richard AP Mathews (5717)
Tony (5408) & Yvonne Mauger
The late WF Mauger (3483) &
    Carolyn Rebstein (née Mauger)
The Very Revd K Paul Mellor,
    Dean of Guernsey
David Millar (10204)
David C Moore (6545)
JJL Morgan (6960)
Daniel Moyles (9884)
John Nelson (7018)
Mark Nightingale (6382)
Alan WH Nicolle (4554)
The family of the late Bernard
    Wrixton Nicolle (4054)
Andrew J Niles (7423)
MG Norman (4697)
Andrew O'Neill (7447)
JRW Ovenden (7671)
David Ozanne (5313)
Benjamin Paine (7552)
John (8192), Trystan (9992),
    Lucas (10206), Griffin (10504)
    and Lachlan (10729) Perkins
Roger Perrot (5450)
Lieutenant Colonel JKR Porter (5482)
IR Priaulx (4562)
The late DL Purdy (5672)
Peter Radford (6386)

The Rt Revd Nicholas Reade (5688)
Advocate Mike Riddiford (6825)
George A Riley (5858)
MG Roberts (5267)
St John A Robilliard (5765)
Alexander Rose (4704)
John Ross (5028)
Sir Geoffrey Rowland (5603)
Angus Sanderson (10808)
Peter Sandwith (9748)
D Neville Scott (5364)
Neville R Scott (4485)
Charlotte, Sophie &
    Jack (10320) Smart
Bruce McL Spittal (7040)
John F Spittal (6967)
John G Stranger (4669)
Major James Symes MC (3967)
Andreas (6968), Peter (10220),
    Andrew (10219) &
    Jacques (10733) Tautscher
Charlie Thompson (10677)
Mark Thompson (6904)
Will Thompson (10871)
Bernard W Thoumine (4526)
Dr Peter Tooley (4740)
Maxwell John Trouteaud (4760)
Rafael (10334) & Mischa (10687)
    Van den Bossche
Simon Walpole (7630)
Alexander LN Watson (9888)
The late Colonel CJ Wetherall (4133)
The late NL Wetherall (3255)
The late Colonel RMG Wetherall
    (3216)
SA Wetherall (7994)
TA Wetherall (5280)
Richard Wheadon
Henri Whitehorne (10737)
Samuel H Williams (9509)
Major John Willis (6212)
Sam Willis (9027)
David (Willy) Wilson (5853)
Martin J (8251) &
    Elliot WA (10793) Wilson
Peter K Wilson (5210)
Toby Wright (9655)
David B Young (5084)

NON SINE SOLE
IRIS.

1

ELIZABETH'S FOUNDATION

'Concerning the school of Her Majesty Queen Elizabeth … I do not know what to say except they hold this great endowment in contempt.'

ADRIAN SARAVIA, FIRST MASTER OF ELIZABETH COLLEGE, IN A LETTER TO SIR WILLIAM CECIL, ON THE PEOPLE OF GUERNSEY

FOUR AND A HALF centuries ago, the religious struggle which had already destroyed the unity of Christendom in Europe was still tearing communities apart in England. For Queen Elizabeth I and her ministers, the Channel Islands were particularly troublesome, partly because of their proximity to Catholic France. Dissidents in Guernsey who were refusing to espouse the Protestant cause had to be reined in. In short, island children were in need of an education at senior or secondary level and for that a school was required. One appalling event in the island became the catalyst of the decision to establish a school that was to take the monarch's name, 'Queen Elizabethe's Grammer Schole', now Elizabeth College, Guernsey.

Elizabeth I: The Rainbow Portrait, c. 1600, attributed to Isaac Oliver.

Part of the Guernsey Millennium Tapestry illustrating 1000 years of local history in ten panels. Here, the burning at the stake of the Cauches family is depicted, with Dr Adrian Saravia on the left holding a book.

the Dean and the Jurats of Guernsey's Royal Court had all connived in an act which was nothing short of barbarism.

Such was the awfulness of the Guernsey execution that an account of it found a place in John Foxe's *Book of Martyrs*, a lavish volume with woodcut illustrations which had become a handbook for opinion-forming Protestants of the Elizabethan age. Foxe described the Guernsey perpetrators as 'this graceless generation of popish tormentors … none more cruel or lacking in compassion'.

What had taken place in Guernsey had become well known in later Elizabethan court circles. Bailiff Gosselin was sacked, seven Jurats were summoned to London and they, too, were sacked. Countless other outrages and frauds by the island authorities were also being uncovered by the Queen's Commissioners and a wholesale investigation was launched into the abysmal administration of the island, both civil and religious.

The comprehensive enquiry of 1824 into the 'State and Condition of Elizabeth College' summarised the social deprivations that existed in the late 1500s and early 1600s, when Elizabeth College was established by royal command:

In 1556, three Guernsey women, Catherine Cauches and her two daughters, Perotine and Guillemine, were burned at the stake. The accusation against them was simply one of theft but, by a gross twisting and manipulation of court procedure and practice, they were actually found guilty of heresy. Compared with the wholesale persecution of other Protestants in mainland England, under the monstrous Mary Tudor, the sentences handed down to the Cauches family in Guernsey were not all that extraordinary. Hundreds had met similar fates, including the Archbishop of Canterbury, Thomas Cranmer.

What was particularly horrifying in the Cauches case, however, was that young Perotine was pregnant. As the flames engulfed the three women, Perotine gave birth to a baby son. The baby was saved by an onlooker, but the then Bailiff of Guernsey, Helier Gosselin, appears to have declared that the boy must be guilty, by association, and should die with his mother, grandmother and aunt. The baby was mercilessly lobbed back into the fire. The Bailiff,

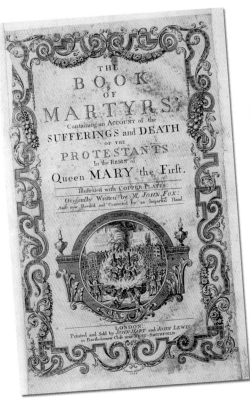

Frontispiece of John Foxe's *Book of Martyrs*.

College titles

Many names have been given to Elizabeth I's foundation. What started as 'Queen Elizabethes Grammer Schole' became 'Le College de notre Souverayne Dame La Royne', 'Grande Eschole de la Royne', 'Ecole Elisabeth' and on the 1824 re-chartering foundation stone 'The School of Elizabeth ... now called the Royal College of Elizabeth'. For many years it has simply been known as Elizabeth College, Guernsey and in the island itself as 'The College' or simply 'College'.

The island ... appears to have been most deplorable, for ignorance, superstition, and, especially, for the unsettled state of its political and religious affairs. The terror of Queen Mary's reign had been exercised here as well as in the mother country. In the year of the institution of the College, three persons were burned for witchcraft ... the whole island was in a state of dissension and confusion.

In 1563, the Privy Council had decided Guernsey was more than ready for reform. The Council's recommendation to examine the island's 'spiritual and temporal jurisdictions ... to reform errors and abuses' came hand in hand with the resolution to establish Elizabeth College by Royal Charter. The Charter required the States to 'erect a free grammar school called "Queene Elizabethes Grammer Schole" under the seal of the isle: the schoolmaster thereof to be appointed and removable by the captain [Governor of Guernsey] except the queen shall otherwise order: the school to be endowed with wheat rents of 80 quarters a year'.

The foundation of the College had thus become a major part of the planned reforms to rid the island of the religious mayhem that had persisted for half a century and more. For the first time, young men of the island would be educated and grounded properly in Protestantism, some of whom, it was hoped, would become island clergymen.

The Patent Rolls, a record of government business, housed at the National Archives in Kew. Instead of records in book form, separate sheets were stitched together into long rolls, one for each year. The intention to set up Elizabeth College is recorded on this roll.

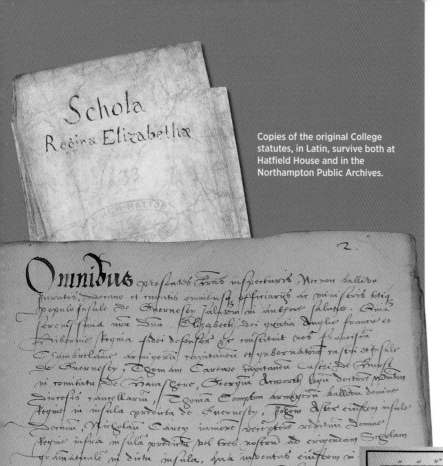

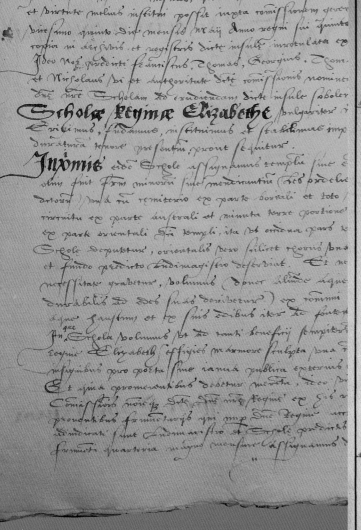

Dr Darryl Ogier, Guernsey's archivist, says that although the death of Mary in 1558 proved the fatal blow to Catholicism in Guernsey, the shape of the island's religious organisation was relatively slow to emerge. Nevertheless, the Commission of 1563 did have an island-wide effect and not only established the College, but also seized and redistributed large amounts of Catholic property. Dr Ogier thinks it entirely plausible that Queen Elizabeth would personally have approved the foundation of the College. A copy of the College statutes, held by Hatfield House in Hertfordshire, is signed off by the Queen's Chief Minister, the all-powerful

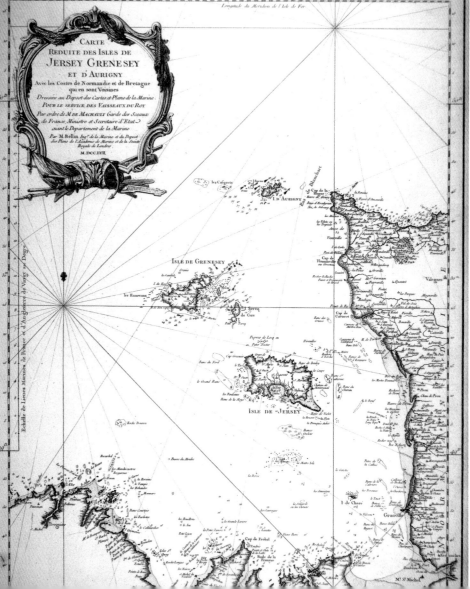

Above: The Coat of Arms of Elizabeth I, above the main door of the College, the dragon and the lion showing Elizabeth was Queen of England and of Wales. Her personal motto, not on these Royal Arms, *Semper Eadem* (Always the Same), is the motto of the College.

Below: Sir William Cecil, Elizabeth I's favourite courtier and Chief Minister, was closely associated with the foundation of the College.

William Cecil. Hatfield's archivist, Robin Harcourt Williams, says this would have happened only with the knowledge and agreement of the Queen.

The statutes set out in detail the area of land that was to be made available for the establishment of the school – land which has been occupied by the College ever since: 'We give, assign and concede for ever, to the said School, the Temple or Church, which formerly belonged to the Minor or Mendicant Friars [Les Cordeliers] together with the burying ground to the Northward.' The original grant of land was later modified and subsequent ownership and responsibility much disputed.

The statutes were also quite specific about the duties of both the Master and the boys, and what was required of the island authorities. However, the first recommendation appears never to have been fulfilled, 'that the statue of Queen Elizabeth, carved in marble, together with the arms of the Sovereigns of England, be placed externally, at the public gate or door of the school'.

No evidence exists that there was ever a statue of Queen Elizabeth anywhere in the island, let alone at the gate of the school she founded. The 1824 Committee of Enquiry highlighted the missing statue and coat of arms: 'The Committee have searched for these objects but find only the arms over the great gate without a vestige or appearance of a statue having ever been there erected.' The Royal Coat of Arms has been proudly displayed over the main door of the present building since at least the 1930s.

For would-be Masters (later Principals) of the new foundation, the qualities demanded by the 1563 Commissioners suffered no lack of clarity: 'Let some fit Master be chosen, with good morals, noted for the infamy of no evident crime and … grave in countenance and deportment.'

A Master would be sacked by the Governor of the island 'if he shall be intolerably cruel towards the Scholars … or shall offend in graver crimes, such as theft, homicide, perjury, heresy, fornication, adultery, drunkenness or gluttony'.

The statutes list the main authors to be read by pupils: Virgil, Horace, Livy, Caesar, Herodotus: 'In the afternoon hours, let them read the Epistles of Cicero, which they call familiar.' Some light relief was offered, in their eyes, from this deathly syllabus. The Master could 'add something of his own to sharpen the wits of the Scholars and allow some singing, arithmetic and writing'.

Queen Elizabeth was fluent in Latin, French, Italian, Spanish and Greek, wrote impeccable English and was taught by one of the most able Greek scholars in England, Roger Ascham. This was Her Majesty's new college and the syllabus reflected that. On the face of it, with generous grants of land and income ordered by the Privy Council, all was set fair for a flourishing school on the lines of several similar establishments which had successfully existed in England for some time.

The appointment of a distinguished scholar, Adrian Saravia, as the school's first Master was further proof that the new foundation had the blessing and support of influential clerics in the Church of England, such as John Whitgift, the Archbishop of Canterbury, one of Saravia's friends.

And yet, just two years after the College had received its Royal Charter, members of the Privy Council, meeting at

Legge's survey of the Channel Islands, 1680.
Castle Cornet was separated from St Peter
Port until the mid-nineteenth century.

right. If one happens to go to a church in the country to
preach a sermon, one is received with laughter and
giggling; nor does their outrageous behaviour stop here,
for they fill the pulpit with foul-smelling dung. Religion
is despised or neglected; here it is permitted without fear
of punishment to rob, to injure the innocent, to kill
someone. I am not saying laws are being broken, since
they have none ... those who are called Jurats tyrannise
the people as if they were dumb animals.

Concerning the school of Her Majesty Queen
Elizabeth ... I do not know what to say except they hold
this great endowment in contempt. None of those things
which were decreed by the Queen's Commissioners
have been put into effect. This uncivilised race hates
all learning.

In a second letter to Sir William Cecil, a year later, Saravia
sees no future for Elizabeth College: 'My lord, about the
people here I write nothing except that they will never
change. Farewell.'

Sir Francis Chamberlayne, Guernsey's Governor,
pleaded with Cecil to persuade Saravia to stay in Guernsey as
Master of the College, 'for the instruction of youth in good
letters, and also for the setting forth of good and sound
doctrine, whereof there is no little want here'.

The plea fell on deaf ears. It's not certain when Saravia
left the island but contemporary records in Southampton
suggest he had become headmaster of the city's King Edward
VI School in 1571. Not only that, Saravia had taken two
promising Guernsey scholars with him, Nicollas Effard and
Nicollas Careye, in the hope that they could be awarded
scholarships to Oxford and Cambridge. It could not have
been a worse start for Elizabeth College and it took a further
two and a half centuries before the school had proper
buildings and a half-competent staff: during that time, the
pupil roll never rose above 30.

Why the larger of the two main Channel Islands,
Jersey, was nearly three centuries behind its sister in
establishing a grammar school has never been satisfactorily
answered. In his *History of Guernsey*, Jonathan Duncan
suggested that the Queen looked favourably on Guernsey,
'she being very closely connected with the ancestors of the
present Carey family, so numerous and respectable in
the island'.

Windsor, felt compelled to write to the Guernsey
authorities complaining that even though the Queen had
'so graciously and liberally bestowed a house and revenue
for the maintenance of a Schoolmaster for the teaching of
the young', they had contributed nothing whatsoever
towards the project. The Council warned that the lack of
action might 'happily move Her Majesty' to divert the
promised funding elsewhere.

In a long and detailed letter to Sir William Cecil, Saravia
had catalogued what he saw as the pervasive evils that
poisoned life in Guernsey. His comments could hardly have
been more damning:

This people is made up totally of cheats and liars ...
everything is judged by a calculation of personal advantage
or disadvantage rather than on grounds of what is fair and

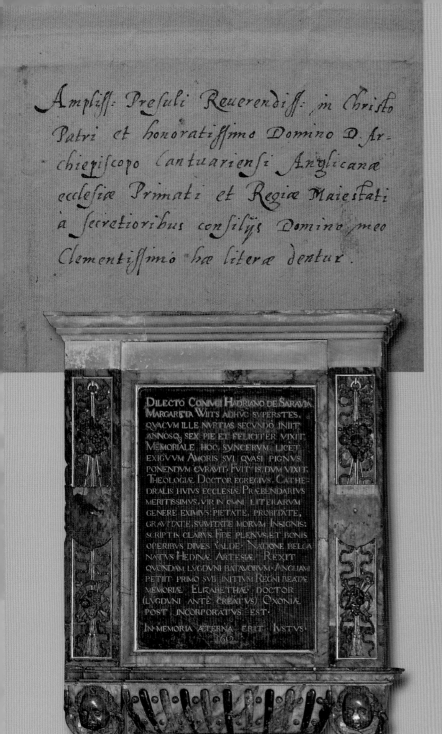

Ampliss: Presuli Reuerendiss: in Christo Patri et honoratissimo Domino D. Archiepiscopo Cantuariensi Anglicanæ ecclesiæ Primati et Regiæ Maiestati à secretioribus consilijs Domino meo Clementissimo hæ literæ dentur.

Dr Adrian Saravia

Adrian Saravia is also referred to variously as Hadrian, Hadriano, Hadrian à, Hadrianus Soravius, Adrianus Zaraphya, Adryan Surravia and Adrianus Saravis van Hesdin, the latter confirming his birthplace as Hesdin, then part of Flanders, now a commune in northern France.

He was a member of the Dutch Church in London and founder of the Walloon Church in Antwerp. His time at Elizabeth College was followed by a headmastership in Southampton and a professorship at Leiden University. He was nominated as one of the translators of the King James Bible, the 400th anniversary of which was much celebrated in 2011. Saravia and his group of fellow translators were given responsibility for the *Old Testament* books of 'Genesis' to 'Kings II'. Saravia himself was said to have been the only translator who was not English. He was made a canon of Canterbury Cathedral and an inscription in the north aisle of the nave marks his death in 1613: 'He was a distinguished Doctor of Theology, an outstanding man in all branches of letters, remarkable for the piety, uprightness, sobriety and sweetness of his conduct, renowned for his writings, full of faith and abounding richly in good works.'

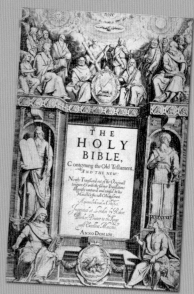

Above left: An envelope, in Saravia's hand, addressed to 'the most honourable and most reverend … Lord Archbishop of Canterbury …'. It contained a letter to John Whitgift, Saravia's good friend.

Left: The inscription over Saravia's tomb in Canterbury Cathedral.

Right: Saravia was one of the translators of the King James Bible.

Hadrianus Sarravia

When Elizabeth became Queen, wrote Duncan, she didn't forget her cousins and appointed one of them, Nicholas Carey, as a Commissioner responsible for the foundation of the College. 'The Careys are the only family in the island who can connect themselves with the blood royal of England.'

A decade later, Ferdinand Tupper, in his own *History of Guernsey*, poured scorn on these claims. 'The Careys never had the most distant connection with the blood royal of England … no more so than any Irish serf of the same name.' Guernsey's upper classes such as the Careys were no more than 'what in England would be termed the middle orders of society'.

Elizabeth I almost certainly did propose a foundation in Jersey, but the allocation of money was used for other purposes. In 1610, James I decreed that the 'foundation of the said Elizabeth College, Jersey, hath been utterly neglected and the revenues put to other uses'. Where Jersey had failed, Guernsey had succeeded – but only just. There were rough times ahead.

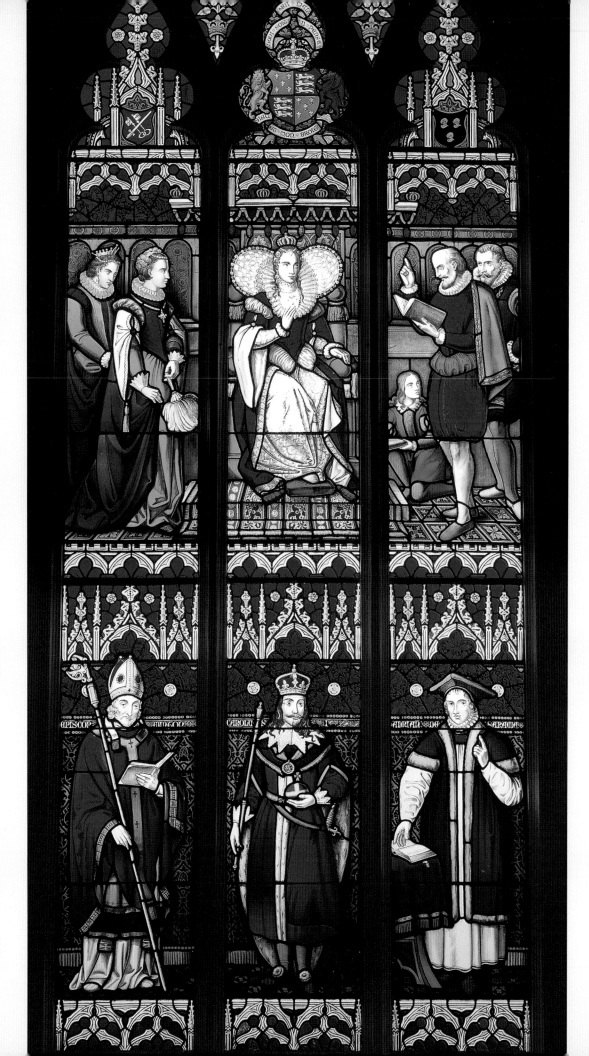

The stained glass window in the College Hall showing Queen Elizabeth and her courtiers. Bishop Morley, King Charles I and Dr Saravia occupy the lower panes.

2

MASTERLY FAILURE

'Mr Nicholas Carey, the Master, appears to imagine that the conditions on which he holds his appointment do not compel him to enter the school as an instructor.'

Sir John Colborne, Lt Governor of Guernsey

For the many reasons that are now all too clear, Elizabeth College tottered on the brink of extinction for two and a half centuries. The States of Guernsey were never sure where their responsibilities lay towards the foundation, nor whether they should be acting as quasi-Trustees; the statutes had not made clear how and at whose expense the buildings were to be maintained; no rules on how the Master should be appointed had been established; the financial security of the school, in the hands of nobody in particular, was, at best, shaky.

If sixteenth-century England was mature enough to nurture the many earlier grammar schools established by Tudor monarchs, the Channel Islands were certainly not. Much as it may injure the pride of old and present Elizabethans, the story of Elizabeth College in the two and a

Old College, now the Ozanne Building, built in 1760.

College land seizure

When the land and buildings of the first friary site were abandoned, the area was treated as wasteland and filched by some of the island's well-to-do families. Even Lt Governors were implicated in the illegal seizure of College property, as the later 1824 Committee of Enquiry was to make clear. As the Committee had been set up by the then Lt Governor himself, Sir John Colborne, any effort by the College to regain ownership of land seized by previous Lt Governors was tricky, to say the least. It was hardly surprising that the language used to address Sir John on the subject was excessively obsequious: 'The Committee, having clearly shown that the spot now occupied by His Excellency the Lt Governor's stables is precisely the site of the Temple and Edifices first assigned for the School and its Master, would suggest that it might be submitted to His Excellency, with deference and respect ... that he may be pleased in due time, if he thinks it necessary ... to restore the land to the College.'

His Excellency was having none of it.

In a letter to the Bailiff, Sir John wrote: 'A great part of the endowment of Elizabeth College lands was illegally transferred, not many years after it had

Portrait of Sir John Colborne, Lt Governor, in the Le Marchant Room. His sons were OEs 1 and 2.

been delivered over to the States. But as the States and authorities ... probably connived at numerous unwarrantable proceedings, and as the lands have been lost to the College for more than two centuries, the present possessors of the property in question ... could not, with any justice, be called on to surrender it.'

half centuries post-1563 turns out to be one which centres on neglect of buildings, alienated lands and principals who were both incompetent and uncommitted. One after another, they were either dismissed or resigned following acrimonious disputes with the authorities.

The ordinary people of Guernsey, increasingly wishing to have their sons educated in the island and not across the Channel in England, were beginning to demand a properly run Elizabeth College. The official enquiry in 1824 recorded 'many instances of complaints against the masters of the school for neglect of duty and for incompetency … the instruction has, from its first establishment, been very irregularly and imperfectly given'.

From the outset, most arguments between the school and island authorities were about pupil accommodation and responsibility for the upkeep of the buildings. What was hardly ever disputed was how they were to be taught. Perhaps the biggest concern for the College staff was how much profit they could make out of their pupil boarders.

Many questions remain unanswered about the size, the exact position of the early College buildings and the extent of the land on which they stood. It is known that three separate establishments were used as the main school before 1829, the year the present College was completed. Premises off the college site were also requisitioned from time to time

as classrooms. The grant of 1563, to support the foundation of the College, was a small parcel of land where the friary church, or 'temple', stood. That building, or part of it, became the first 'school of Elizabeth' — the original friary had closed 30 years earlier after confiscation by the Crown.

In 1568, the College was awarded a second grant which took in the rest of the friary grounds — a gift from the Queen and Privy Council of 'all the land within the friary close, including a house, for the use and benefit of the

View of Castle Cornet and St. Peter Port, circa 1680, by an unknown artist from the circle of Peter Monamy.

22

Left: The only visible remains of the original friary buildings and the College Gateway at the lower end of College Street. Other remnants were probably knocked down when St Julian's Avenue was created in the 1870s.

Right: Plan drawn by John Wilson showing the boundaries of land assigned to the College since the Foundation and prior to the construction of the 1829 building.

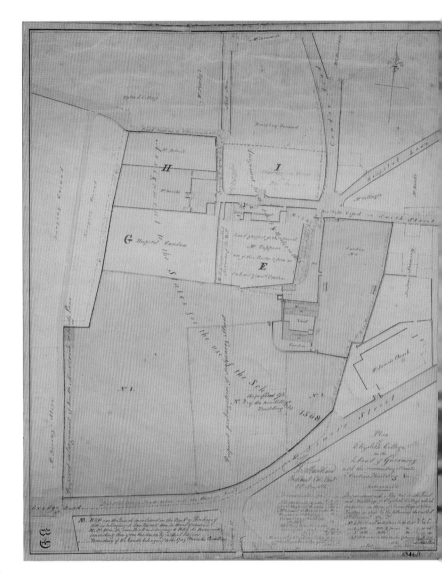

Grammar School of Queen Elizabeth with £20 sterling for the repair of the house'. The enlarged College site then became roughly as it is now, enclosed by Upland Road, part of Monument Gardens, Rue des Frères, College Street and the Grange, although these particular thoroughfares are much changed today.

Soon after the 1568 Privy Council order was made, the College moved from its adapted temple to this second friary property. Twenty years later, the States converted the schoolhouse into a temporary prison: the 1590 plague had either made regular class attendance by pupils impossible or had simply put an end to it altogether. Whichever was the case, it only served to underline the parlous state into which the College as an institution was spiralling.

In 1753, the house that had been school, then prison, then school again was decreed dilapidated and too costly to repair and demolished by order of the States. Its replacement, in 1760, was the first purpose-built school on the site and for nearly 70 years it provided classrooms and living accommodation for the Master and space for boys' dormitories. This same building, with later modifications (the Ozanne Building), now houses the Maths department and Design Technology workshops.

The new Elizabeth College in the 1760s had been perceived as the dawn of a changed era for island education, but it proved another false one. There was little, if any, improvement. School numbers remained ridiculously low — precious few day pupils and even fewer boarders. The

Masters for those 70 years after 1760 were to continue with the greed, absenteeism and pluralism of their forebears in the previous two centuries.

THE MASTERS 1563–1759

The complete succession of Masters after Adrian Saravia in 1563 is difficult to establish with any certainty. The compilers of the Register, Volume 1, produced a list researched from various public documents, but Royal Court records suggest there may be omissions. In any event, the roll is hardly one of honour, although there are notable exceptions, some of whom were distinguished academics such as Isaac Basire (1638–1639), a highly regarded and much-travelled priest who later became chaplain to Charles I and, following the restoration of the monarchy, to Charles II.

Castle Cornet, pre-1672 when the tower was destroyed by a gunpowder explosion. The castle was often used as a prison for victims of religious intolerance, including the three Cauches women accused of heresy.

Sir John Colborne

Sir John Colborne, soldier and colonial administrator, led the charge which routed Napoleon's Old Guard in the Battle of Waterloo. When he became Lt Governor of Guernsey, he preoccupied himself with education, in particular the revival of the College, and island road links. One of the main roads out of St Peter Port bears his name. He later became Lt Governor of Upper Canada and Commander in Chief of North America before being promoted to Field Marshal and then raised to the peerage as Baron Seaton. A statue of Colborne is to be found at the Peninsula Barracks in Winchester.

Adrian Saravia was respected by his fellow academics and certainly well connected with civil and church leaders of the day, but his tenure of the Mastership was inauspicious. Any sort of prominence achieved by his immediate successors was mostly as a result of scandals, blatant fraud or complete inadequacy. Martin de Pestere, Master in 1574, was connected with a case of infanticide: he was required to leave the College in 1607. Several subsequent Masters were unable to converse in French, as required by the statutes, and dismissed. A petition from parents was raised against William Johnson (1682–1698) and the Dean of Guernsey upheld their complaints: 'Upon examination, Mr Johnson has been found incapable of translating Latin into French or of correcting the scholars in so doing.'

The subject of repairs to College buildings appears regularly in Royal Court records and for many years it was the only aspect of the school in which the States took much interest. George Delgarno was Master on two separate occasions, having once resigned after the Royal Court told him to pay for building repairs himself. Delgarno's successor, Gabriel du Perier, had his own income reduced after a similar ruling.

A petition from islanders in 1639 to have Jacob de l'Espine sacked was ignored by the Lt Governor, but the States appear to have dismissed him anyway for 'négligence et autre mépris de ses devoirs' – dereliction of duty. College Masters were not immune from English politics – Nicholas Carey was appointed Master in 1645 but as a committed Parliamentarian, he was ousted when the monarchy was restored in 1660.

In 1711, there were calls for the Revd Lawrence Payne's dismissal on the grounds of his 'neglect for several years of the education of the youth and for his absence from the school'. Payne was away in England for 18 months while still claiming a salary as Master.

THE MASTERS 1760–1824

The new school building and the promise of a new order only ushered in old practices. John Hemming had become both Master of the College and Dean of Guernsey, but he refused to open the new school until the States recovered the lands alienated from the College in the past. Ignoring a summons to appear before the Royal Court, Hemming claimed it had no jurisdiction over him as Master. 'If there be any complaint to be made against the Master of Elizabeth College, let it be legally done: first to the Dean and then to the Right Honourable the Governor.' In other words, he himself, as Dean, should judge any complaint. Eventually, Hemming opened the school, but with only a few scholars.

The Revd Elias Crespin, appointed in 1761, stayed, nominally, as Master for 34 years but often employed assistants in his absence. The only missing malpractice in the appointment system was nepotism. It arrived when Dean Crespin resigned in 1795 to secure the Mastership for his nephew, the Revd Nicholas Carey. Carey was Master for nearly 30 years and his appalling record during that time was the last straw which persuaded the Royal Court to sanction an official enquiry into the state of Elizabeth College.

Exchanges of letters in 1821 between the Lt Governor, the Dean and the Master are astonishing. Sir John Colborne asked Dean Durand whether Elizabeth College could ever be a fit place of education for the sons of the inhabitants of Guernsey with 'the statutes totally neglected and the intentions of the Foundress frustrated. Mr Nicholas Carey, the Master, appears to imagine that the conditions on which he holds his appointment do not compel him to enter the school as an instructor'.

Left: The Revd
Nicholas Carey.

Below: The Ozanne
building, watercolour,
1888.

Asked to give some account of the number of boys on the register during his tenure, it is difficult to decide whether Carey was just arrogant or simply ignorant of what was required from a Master.

> In regard to the number of scholars I have had, I cannot answer to this question with the exact precision I could wish, but will do it cheerfully and conscientiously to the best of my knowledge. From April 1795 to nearly the same period 1798, the average number of boys has been 15 or 16; but towards the middle of this year, the school became in a very languid state and in 1799, I do not believe there was one boy. However, in January 1800, the school greatly revived, and the number of scholars amounted to 18, which continued to 1806; from that period to January 1816, the establishment again became very low, frequently only one or two boys, and indeed, the three later years, say from January 1813 to 1816, no boys at all.

On Carey's attendance figures, probably inflated anyway, fewer than 200 boys went through the school over a period of 30 years – an average of seven a year.

When the text of the 1824 enquiry was published, even the foreword by the committee chairman, Major TF de Havilland, was damning of 'the irregularities and abuses which have pervaded every department of Elizabeth College … an establishment originally imperfect and ill-suited to the community which for centuries past has proved of little use'.

Major de Havilland complained to his readers that the committee 'scarcely knew where to look for documents of any description, since no record had been kept at the College and we have therefore had to trace our way in the dark'.

The 1824 enquiry report only confirmed what was already known about the College and was in the public domain. In his *History of Guernsey* in 1815, the respected historian William Berry condemned the school as a complete waste of money. 'This excellent institution is no longer of the service intended and the revenue might now be more charitably disposed of. The Mastership is a sinecure appointment, there being seldom more than two or three boys attending, and often none.'

Although it had been virtually impossible to remove Nicholas Carey as Master against his will, a deal was done with the States. 'Arrangements have been made with the Revd Nicholas Carey by which, in consideration of a pension of £60 per annum, he abandons his rights to the enjoyment of the buildings, lands, and rentes of Elizabeth College.'

Nicholas Carey's demise signalled the end of the old order. Ahead lay a renaissance, all due to a small band of visionaries headed by Sir John Colborne.

3

THE RENAISSANCE

'The time is not far distant, placed as the island is in the centre of Europe, when pupils will flock to Guernsey, not only from all parts of the British empire, but from other surrounding nations.'

DANIEL DE LISLE BROCK, BAILIFF OF GUERNSEY

*I*T WAS A CELEBRATION unequalled in the history of Guernsey, an occasion of such splendour that, even if King George himself had been present, it could hardly have been grander. The Royal College of Elizabeth was to be reborn in a magnificent new building: it would be the biggest single-building project ever undertaken in the island.

The laying of the foundation stone of the new Elizabeth College in 1826 would mark the beginning of its renaissance — an act of faith by the States of Guernsey and the population of the island.

The Elizabeth College of today would never have survived at all but for the vision of a small band of dedicated men who took on the Herculean task of education reform in Guernsey in the 1820s. Although Sir John Colborne as

South elevation of Elizabeth College by the architect John Wilson.

George Le Boutillier

George Le Boutillier came to Guernsey from Jersey when he was 21, set up a drapery business in the town and took a great interest in local politics. He had four sons, hence his interest in educational improvements. George and his brother, James, were responsible for the creation of the Commercial Arcade, previously known as Le Boutillier's Arcade. The project involved quarrying and moving 120,000 cartloads of stone and gravel which were dumped on what is now the South Esplanade. The scheme, though successful, was never quite finished and became a financial disaster for the Le Boutilliers: the *Gazette de Guernesey*, however, said that before the brothers came on the scene, St Peter Port was 'a nut without a kernel'. The family emigrated to America and set up hugely popular and flourishing department stores in Philadelphia and New York. The *College Register* describes George Le Boutillier as 'one of the greatest benefactors that ever came to this island'.

Above: **Le Boutillier Bros trade card, 1880s.**

Right: **George Le Boutillier.**

Report of Committee of Enquiry into the state of Elizabeth College, 1824.

ENQUIRY INTO THE PRESENT STATE AND CONDITION OF ELIZABETH COLLEGE, AT GUERNSEY; THROUGH THE MEANS OF A COMMITTEE APPOINTED BY His Excellency Colonel Sir John Colborne, K.C.B. THE LIEUTENANT-GOVERNOR, WITH THE CONCURRENCE OF THE ROYAL COURT.

PRINTED AND PUBLISHED FOR GENERAL INFORMATION, WITH HIS EXCELLENCY'S SANCTION.

GUERNSEY: PRINTED BY N. MAUGER, PRINTER TO THE KING'S MOST EXCELLENT MAJESTY, BORDAGE-STREET, TOP OF FOUNTAIN-STREET. 1824.

Lt Governor was the figurehead, it was a Jersey businessman, George Le Boutillier, who was mainly responsible for starting the process which rescued the school from certain oblivion. The painstaking 1824 official enquiry was set up as a direct result of Le Boutillier's plans for the complete reform of the College.

The enquiry committee put forward no fewer than 79 proposals for the reforms of Elizabeth College. These included:

- Setting up a body of Trustees (now the Board of Directors) and a completely new set of rules governing the appointment and conduct of the Master – now to become 'the Principal'.
- The number of boys not to exceed 150.
- No provision to be made for the opposite sex. (Girls had been expressly included in the original statutes.)
- The age of admission to be from 8 to 14 years – no boy to remain after the age of 19.
- The Principal should be a middle-aged man.
- Latin and Greek should continue to be taught as before, as well as the English classics, general history, elocution and *Belles Lettres*. All classes to be taught French, navigation, trigonometry, geography, the use of globes and surveying, book-keeping, algebra, mensuration and civil engineering.
- Holidays to be a month at Christmas and at midsummer, a week at Easter.
- Queen Elizabeth's statue to be erected, as prescribed by the Royal Commissioners in 1563.
- The construction of new buildings.

Portrait of the Revd Charles Stocker from the Le Marchant Room Collection.

The last of these would take five years, but the enquiry committee lost no time in pressing ahead with immediate reform. By October 1824, the Revd Dr Charles Stocker had been appointed Principal, bringing with him, as Vice-Principal, the Revd William Davies, a colleague and friend, both fellows of St John's, Oxford, and distinguished academics in their own fields.

Temporary accommodation, 'two well-lighted rooms, fifty-seven feet in length', had been obtained in the New Street/Berthelot Street area, close enough to the existing College site, and the school was ready for business with no fewer than 43 boys enrolled. The Lt Governor, Sir John Colborne, opened the new schoolrooms with a speech which justified, in the strongest terms, plans for the future.

'It has been said that a new College is not required here. I have never known a place where it was more wanted', said Sir John, adding that the accents of Guernsey boys might be shaken off by the appointment of 'French masters from France and English masters from England'. Such a remark would not have been well received today, but his suggestion struck a chord with the examiners in 1829, who noted that recitation 'was quite free from local inaccuracies or peculiarities of accent'.

The new premises were unquestionably spartan, but the Bailiff, Daniel de Lisle Brock, brimming with optimism, hoped the time was not far distant when pupils would flock to Guernsey, 'not only from all parts of the British empire, but from other surrounding nations'.

Henry Tupper, Jurat of the Royal Court, 1857–1875.

Frederick Corbin Lukis, founder of the Lukis Collection and father of OEs 26, 54, 55 and 599.

Widespread initial support for this bold new venture was demonstrated by the willingness of Guernsey's old-established families to have their sons educated under the changed regime. Their names appear on the opening pages of the first official register of pupils.

James and Francis Colborne, the two sons of the Lt Governor, were first. George Le Boutillier's three sons, Charles, George and James (and Thomas, later), came after the Colbornes, followed by a list which included names from some of Guernsey's best-known families: Le Mottée, Carey, de Havilland, Tupper, de Sausmarez, Guille and Maingy.

The Colbornes, who stayed five years at the College while their father was Lt Governor, subsequently had distinguished careers themselves. James Colborne (1) became a Major-General and ADC to his father, by then the Governor-General of Canada. Francis Colborne (2) also became an army general and was knighted.

The Le Boutillier brothers all emigrated to the United States with their father and founded Le Boutillier's in New York. Most of the boys in that small first intake went on to make significant contributions to life both in Guernsey and elsewhere, such as: Henry Tupper (17), a lawyer and Jurat of the Royal Court, whose energies led to the construction of

Daniel de Lisle Brock, Bailiff of Guernsey 1821–1842, one of Guernsey's most able Bailiffs and a devoted supporter of the College.

the Hanois Lighthouse, the new harbours of St Peter Port and St Sampson, the breakwater at Saints Bay, St Julian's Avenue and the New Markets. Tupper's uncles were Daniel de Lisle Brock, Bailiff, and Sir Isaac Brock, 'who saved Canada for the Empire'. Charles de Havilland (14) became a Maths master at the College before going on to teach at Eton; Thomas Lacy (16), an army doctor, became Deputy Inspector-General of hospitals; Havilland de Sausmarez (21), a Cambridge scholar, became bursar and fellow of Pembroke College, Oxford; Havilland's brother was General George de Sausmarez (101).

George Guille (18) was a Morley Scholar at Pembroke, Oxford; Frederic Lukis (26) trained as a surgeon but was also an antiquarian and a member of the famous Lukis family which did so much for island museums.

Richard Isemonger (28) was a ship owner, John Macqueen (34) a customs officer, Thomas Power (7) a planter in Texas, Henry Carey (12) a wine merchant.

Compared with what had gone before, the achievements of that first intake, admittedly the sons of well-to-do parents, were nothing short of outstanding. By October 1825, Dr Stocker was able to report that in the first year there had been more than 100 boys on the school roll: 'Many of the scholars have greatly distinguished themselves and when questioned, their answers are such as would prove creditable at an examination for a degree at Oxford.'

Stocker had a reputation for unmerciful flogging. Keen to dispel any such impression, his report to the College authorities, however, wasn't exactly convincing: 'I have been anxious gradually to abolish corporal punishment … it appears a much better plan to remove a scholar to a lower form as he is then deterred by shame. Where this system fails … I must resort to the more harsh and disagreeable method of coercion.'

One particular case illustrates how errant pupils could be ruthlessly punished. Hugh Monk, the father of three boys at the College, complained not only to the Directors but to the Lt Governor about injuries to his eldest son's groin: 'I understand the injury inflicted was merely accidental from his writhing while under punishment … but it clearly shows little care was taken where the lash fell. It is unaccountable that for so trifling a complaint, thirty-six lashes should have been given him when the severest punishment is stated by the Master to be only nine or ten lashes.'

William Monk's supposed crime was summarised by his father: 'The boy had taken an egg to school for lunch and by accident it rolled out of his pocket. Dreading the consequences, he tried to conceal it and wipe it up with his pocket handkerchief.' Nothing much came of Mr Monk's complaint and the boy himself (60) went on to become a surgeon, as did his brother Hugh (268). The archives also record an incident when Stocker was approached by a Mr Lukis, who 'on the public road, without any provocation, made use of very improper language towards me, using the epithets of tyrant and good-for-nothing fellow and accusing me of cruel and shameless conduct towards his grandson'.

Such accusations were mostly brushed aside. Stocker and Davies applied themselves to raising the academic standing of the newly established school and it was time, anyhow, to concentrate on the proposed vast new building and how it should be financed. Sir John Colborne, as might have been expected, was eager to trumpet the benefits of a reformed College, its new home and the good it would bring to the island. The community would gain considerably, he said, from the £8,000 spent on the construction of the school. Not only would it encourage parents to send sons over to Guernsey for their education but it would keep boys in the island who might otherwise be sent 'at enormous expense' to England.

Above and left: Names and numbers found in the tower, and carved in the lock-ups.

Below: Remembrance poppies at the Smith Street War Memorial.

School numbers

Whoever decided to allocate numbers to boys as they were entered on the official register cannot possibly have anticipated the consequences. Whereas boys in many schools are identified by name and year of entry or school house, the numbers given to Elizabethans have been their main distinguishing marks since 1824. Name and number are preferred on woven tapes and numbers alone were once punched into the soles of shoes with brass nails.

Amias Andros described the day he joined the school in 1847 in his *Consule Planco* (*The Good Old Days*): 'I passed through the College gates and, penetrating into the Hall, was introduced to Dr Bromby, who

Left: Amias Andros, April 1861, and the title page of *Consule Planco*, 1877.

Below: The first entries in the College Register.

then and there enrolled me as a member of the College and ticketed me Number 878 ... for half a dozen years I was known at the College only by that magic number.'

Many Old Elizabethans (OEs) still greet each other by their numbers and it has become fashionable to use them on car number plates in the island. At auctions of car registrations in Guernsey, four-figure OE numbers are sold at a premium.

For example, TJ de Putron (4482) had his number transferred to a Triumph TR3 in 1969. In 2006, the mother of T Wright (9655) bought her son's number at auction, but he had to wait seven years before he was old enough to take a driving test and use the number on a car. SWF Rebstein (7380) has a car registration he inherited from his grandfather, WF Mauger (3483).

School numbers went into five figures when TW Nightingale (10,000) joined the school in 2002. Tom was presented with a drinking cup and a teddy bear.

Tom Nightingale and Dr Nick Argent, 2002.

Above: The Guernsey Fish Market, built in the 1820s (etching by Barry Owen-Jones) and above right the fish-scale design of the roof.

Below right: George IV.

The Bailiff, Daniel de Lisle Brock, made the boldest of appeals in the chamber of the States to support the financing of the new school: 'One might certainly build a College less spacious and less splendid, at a smaller expense, if the object of the States was to save two or three thousand pounds and erect a school for ten or twelve scholars.' Doing things by halves would be akin to doing nothing at all, he added. 'In that case, we shall have no College — nor one hundred and fifty or two hundred students — nor respectable professors — and thus our object will be defeated, and the confidence of His Majesty's government, and of His Excellency Sir John Colborne, cruelly disappointed.'

Bailiff Brock reminded the States how several people had been opposed to the construction of the new market in Fountain Street, praised afterwards as one of the finest in the whole of Europe. 'With what obstinacy they endeavoured to persuade the States that meat could never be kept fresh in the new market, twenty more times airy than the old one — and alleged a hundred such absurdities. These persons retarded the work for a considerable time, but as soon as the members of the States consulted their own good sense and sound judgement, truth triumphed. The States have recognised … the necessity of building a College; they have asked for means, and his Majesty has graciously given these means, what else remains to be done?'

George IV had issued an Order in Council on 30 September 1825 which allowed the raising of money for the improvement of the College by continuing Guernsey's 1 shilling (5 pence) per gallon tax on spirits. The tax, or *impôt*, would have expired at the end of August 1829, but the Order in Council extended it for a further 15 years. The irony of a new Guernsey school being built and paid for by a tax on alcohol has not been lost on successive generations,

particularly in an island which entered the 21st century with strict Sunday laws forbidding the sale of alcohol in shops and even of petrol at garages on account of its toxicity. The island had another intriguing way of raising capital – literally, printing money. As and when the printed money generated income, the equivalent amount in banknotes was destroyed until the balance was zero. The College was to benefit from this method of tax revenue when the cost of the new building exceeded the original estimate of £8,000. The *Guernsey Star* carried the following description of the laying of the foundation stone on 19 October 1826:

At about half past nine in the morning, the grenadiers and riflemen of each regiment of militia infantry, together with a company of militia artillery, and the buglers of the 81st regiment, assembled at Les Gravées, where they were formed into a brigade. Shortly after ten, the brigade marched towards the Court house, where many of the Constables, the Douzeniers, members of the Court, and clergy, were assembled.

At a quarter before eleven, His Excellency Sir John Colborne arrived; he was accompanied by the Bailiff and the Very Rev the Dean, together with HE's secretary and ADC. HE was saluted by the militia with presented arms – the band and buglers playing 'God Save the King'.

A procession to and from the Town Church was made up in the following order:

– Trumpeters
– A Detachment of the Militia
– Three Pages bearing white rods
– The students of Elizabeth College, two and two, the youngest first
– The Professors, wearing their gowns
– The Principal and Vice-Principal
– The Builder and Master Mason
– The Architect and Clerk
– The Directors of the College
– Band of the Town Regiment
– The States, thus:
– Douzeniers of the parishes
– Constables of the parishes
– Clergy of the island
– The Royal Court, preceded by its officers
– HE The Lt Governor flanked by the Bailiff and the Dean
– A detachment of the Militia

The procession returned up High Street and processed towards the College ground. The number of spectators, which had been but comparatively trifling ... increased considerably as it drew near the College ground. So great was the confusion that nearly half an hour passed before those who were in the rear of the procession, the Douzeniers, the clergy, the Royal Court and the Lt Governor, could enter the ground.

Out of the many thousand persons, perhaps not fifty witnessed the laying of the foundation stone.

A vase containing pieces of the current coins of Great Britain and of France together with pieces of money furnished by various individuals was then deposited in a cavity that had been made in the foundation stone and the hole covered by a brass plate. A small block of granite, suspended over the foundation stone by pullies, was let down upon the plate and cemented with mortar by His Excellency.

Above: Members of Guernsey's Town Militia, 1822.

Below: Government House, aquatint by William Berry, c. 1815.

After the ceremony itself, the College boys were entertained in marquees on the grass outside Government House (now the Old Government House Hotel) and Lady Colborne hosted a grand dinner and ball. The Royal Court and other dignitaries dined at Rossetti's, an eating house where the Guille Allés library now stands. On the New Ground (Cambridge Park) the troops were supplied with wine and biscuits and the workmen were presented with 'a good solid dinner and a hogshead of wine' by the Royal Court.

The party over, the College returned to its temporary rooms and classes. A bright, assured future with a highly qualified staff seemed to lie ahead. With Dr Stocker at the helm, the school would surely establish itself, once and for all, as a worthy community, fit to take possession of its huge new building, the like of which islanders had never seen.

Stocker had taken a full part in the foundation stone-laying and joined in the subsequent celebrations. Not many months later, though, correspondence between him and the Board of Directors revealed that all was not well. After the heady success of 1825 and 1826, the number of new entrants began to decrease – only 20 in 1827 and 17 a year later. The Directors demanded an explanation.

Stocker had already complained of 'the close and confined nature of our present school rooms from which boys are frequently sent home with headaches and complaints of feeling ill'. He had also protested to the Directors that it was impossible for him, Mr Davies and another colleague to teach and listen to scholars all in the same classroom. 'The more we endeavour to remedy the difficulty of hearing, by requiring the boys to raise their voices, the more the evil is increased.' Stocker also surprised the Directors when he indicated he was applying for the post of headmaster at Rugby School.

What, in fact, he was demanding was a pay rise. His main grievance was that under-masters had been allowed to take in boarders and so, his own income reduced, he was unable to make a proper living. 'My friends across the water know my house to be almost empty (of boarders), whereas in England, I could have filled it (charging much higher fees). They are surprised that I persist in remaining where I cannot be making any money and conclude that I must soon be tired of the trial.'

Moreover, Stocker pointed out that the high cost of fitting out rooms at his own expense in the newly constructed College building, with little prospect of attracting fee-paying boarders, had led his friends to suggest he moved back to England.

Stocker acted on their suggestion and resigned.

There were conflicting assessments of him. Christine Ozanne, in her 1926 account of that period, noted that most Guernsey people knew only that Stocker was 'celebrated for unmerciful flogging'. The *Guernsey Star* described him as 'a man of great talent, a strict disciplinarian and punctual to the minute'. That fastidious devotion to punctuality was derided by junior masters, who were fined a shilling for missing prayers and another shilling for every quarter of an hour afterwards.

Above: Classroom in the 1829 building.

Right: Principal Stocker complains of 'close and confined nature' of temporary classrooms, pre-1829.

The Directors had commended Stocker for 'the assiduous care and the ability with which he had reformed the College'.

One eminent parent, Admiral Lord Lyons, was so pleased with the education of his sons that he offered a five-guinea prize for proficiency in Latin. His son, Edmund Lyons (165), subsequently had a distinguished naval career, cut short when he was killed in the Crimean War. His brother, Richard (112), became a British Ambassador, received no fewer than three knighthoods, KCB, GCB and GCMG, and was later ennobled.

Even with successful former pupils such as the Lyons brothers, Dr Stocker's period at the College can only be defined as one of mixed fortunes. The new order had been established, the statutes revised, and there was an excited air of reform and anticipation. The much-needed complete break with the past, however, would come only, it was thought, when boys and staff moved into the new premises.

Stocker's name was on the brass plate covering the foundation stone, but it was Dr George Proctor who walked into the magnificent new College building to take up residence as its first Principal.

Admiral Lord Lyons.

Local opposition

Some Guernsey people were wholly unimpressed by the new school. Alongside the report of the foundation stone ceremony in the *Guernsey Star* was an anonymous 'Letter to the Editor'.

To the Editor of THE STAR.

Sir,—Last Thursday the foundation stone of Elizabeth College was laid by the Lieutenant Governor; half of the douzeniers of the island through whose supposed will the College is to be erected, although invited, did not assemble to enjoy the ceremony, probably through the idea that this institution could not stand many years without further support. The College as it is now managed will take infinitely more to erect than was voted, and the sum voted by the States £10,000 stg. is sufficient to erect a palace, much more a school for education, besides £500 per annum to maintain the incidental expenses which may occur. Now, if we reckon that the establishment has one hundred boys at £12 a year, making £1,200, out of this take £500 for the principal professor, £300 for the second, remains only £400 to pay off the other masters, besides necessary incumbrances. Now, Mr. Editor, from what source must the money come, unless it be by a general taxation? The town parish will then pay one-third of the expenses, and the remainder by all the country parishes; that is to say, the poorest people who cannot afford to put their children in this establishment must pay for its maintenance. If the admirers of learning wished to instruct their fellow ... the blessings of education, why not en-

Richard Lyons and Lyons Medal for Latin.

WILSON'S MAGNUM OPUS

'The present structure, in its utter tastelessness, presents a bald, plastered, unmeaning face.'
DT Ansted and RG Latham, *The Channel Islands*, 1862

'A magnificent College now ornaments the upper part of town.'
Jonathan Duncan, *History of Guernsey*, 1841

'Four grammar schools in different parishes would have done more but the mischief is now done.'
The Guernsey Magazine, 1836

'The building itself is decidedly handsome.'
Henry Inglis, *The Channel Islands*, 1835

'A beautiful specimen of modern, monastic architecture.'
The Strangers' Guide to Guernsey, 1833

'No one can claim its drab Gothic exterior has any architectural merit.'
VG Collenette, Vice-Principal and College historian, 1963

John Wilson came to Guernsey towards the end of the Napoleonic Wars, a clerk of works supervising the building of barracks and fortifications in the island. His skills as a draughtsman and designer were quickly recognised and he soon became the man to whom the States turned for their grand architectural projects.

Elizabeth College by John Wilson, 1830.

Wilson's new Torteval Church.

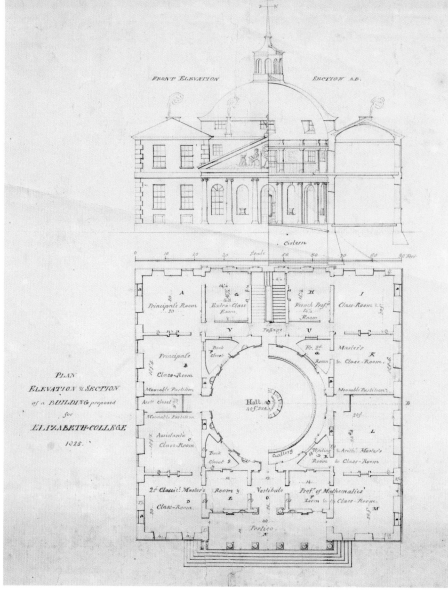

FRONT ELEVATION   SECTION AB.

Cistern

PLAN
ELEVATION & SECTION
of a BUILDING proposed
for
ELIZABETH-COLLEGE
1825.

Above: One of Wilson's alternative plans for the College, and further drawings (above opposite).

Below: Crumbling 'Roman Cement'.

His first assignment was the design and construction of the parish church in Torteval, a distinctive, plain stone building which replaced a crumbling mediaeval edifice. Next on Wilson's drawing board was St James Church in St Peter Port, followed by a portfolio of work for the States, including the fish and meat markets and Fountain Street. He also took on private commissions – Castle Carey, Beau Séjour (the mansion pre-dating the Cambridge Park leisure centre), the Grange Lodge and many other imposing residences for Guernsey's well-to-do.

The new Elizabeth College, however, was to be his finest and grandest achievement in Guernsey and he was disarmingly honoured to have been awarded the contract by the Directors: 'The earnest desire I feel arises not so much from pecuniary motives as from the honest pride I should have in seeing a building of such magnitude finished in a chaste and classical manner under my personal direction.'

Opinions have always varied about the building's aesthetic merits, or lack of them, but no one can deny its

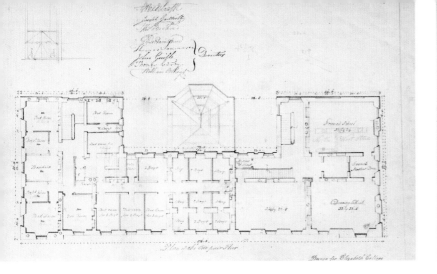
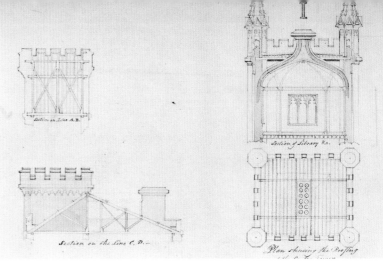

grandeur. A prosaic description was printed in 1834 in *The Graphic and Historical Illustrator*, a construction magazine of the day: 'Its architectural character is appropriate and its internal arrangements are extremely judicious. It forms a parallelogram of two storeys above the basement, is of excellent masonry and considerable extent.' However, the terra cotta Roman Cement, so admired by Wilson and used by him elsewhere in Guernsey, manages to conceal a construction far less solid than at first sight may appear. The walls and foundations are made of rubble, hardly 'excellent masonry', and parts of the turrets are wooden. Successive bursars have shuddered at the very mention of any wholesale renovation of the fabric and the huge costs involved.

Wilson's alternative plans for the new College building, considered and rejected by the Directors, were for a domed building, no less grand in design but slightly smaller in scale. The position of the College on today's St Peter Port skyline would have been equally commanding, but it would certainly have been very different if the Directors had chosen Wilson's alternative drawings.

Elizabeth College and St James still dominate the St Peter Port skyline today.

Admiral James Saumarez

James Saumarez is one of the few OEs known to have been a pupil at the College before the re-chartering in 1824. James and his brother John, sons of Dr Matthew Saumarez of La Plaiderie, are listed as being at the College around 1765 when James would have been eight. He was entered as a midshipman on the books of HMS *Solebay* in 1767, but went to sea in 1769 when he was just 13. In the Royal Navy, the young Saumarez served on various ships at home and in the Mediterranean, including two years on HMS *Victory*. He was knighted after capturing the French frigate, *La Reunion*, in 1793 and was Nelson's second-in-command at the Battle of the Nile in 1798. In command of a small squadron at the Battle of Algeciras in 1801, he routed a far superior combined force of French and Spanish ships. Honours were heaped upon him — a knighthood, a baronetcy and then ennoblement as Baron Saumarez in the Island of Guernsey.

Lord de Saumarez was always a friend of the College and gave great support to those leading the re-chartering: he founded the generous Saumarez Exhibition at the College in 1827 and was instrumental in establishing St James Church. He died in 1836 at his country house in Saumarez Park and is buried in the Castel churchyard.

Remarkably, the huge island construction that stands today was ready to be occupied by students and staff by the summer of 1829, just three years after the laying of its foundation stone. Yet another big celebration was attended by island dignitaries, including Guernsey's most celebrated admiral, Lord de Saumarez.

The new College principal, Dr George Proctor, arrived in Guernsey in time for the grand opening. Proctor, who had been headmaster of Lewes Grammar School in Sussex, had chartered a boat from Newhaven to bring not just his family and furniture to the island, but several new students, many from his previous Sussex school.

One of them was Edward Boys Ellman (219), who gained a First in Maths at Oxford and then spent 66 years as curate and rector of the same parish, Berwick in Sussex. His *Recollections of a Sussex Parson* provide a colourful account of his arrival at the College, just as it began life in its new home: 'On reaching Guernsey, we all stayed at an hotel for three

Right: Edward Boys Ellman.

Below: The Artillery Barracks, Fort George, a lithograph by the College drawing master, Thomas Compton, one of the Moss Print series.

days and fared sumptuously, which hotel was, whilst I was still in Guernsey, burnt down. The new College was not quite completed. Directly the first bedroom could be got finished off, enough to sleep in, five or six of us went in to the top room in the north east tower.'

With his fellow College boarders, Ellman frequently went for early morning swims: 'Our most usual bathing place was a small bay just under the Artillery Barracks at Fort George. Here we were frequently joined by some of the officers from the barracks just above, who came down in their dressing gowns, and afterwards ascended to their own quarters to dress.'

College porter duties

> *Resolved. That the duties of a Porter in the College will be to light and attend the Fires and hot air flues & provide Chips and wood for the purpose at his own expense; to keep the Building (exclusive of the Principals dwelling) completely clean by daily sweeping, and thoroughly washing it at least four times a year, at his own expense as far as regards both labour and materials. That he shall serve the notices & attend on the Board of Directors. Carry any other letters on the service of the College — and the Books which are required for the Scholars. Keep the Gates as required according to the directions he shall receive. Keep the foreground clean. — The whole of his time being entirely at the disposal of the Board of Directors — That he shall sleep in the Lodge that is being built for the Porter and that none of his little Children (if he have any,) shall reside in the Lodge. And that his remuneration shall be Thirty five Pounds & Annum, payable Quarterly.*

An extract from the College Directors' Minutes, 1829.

Elizabeth College, 1880.

members of staff — the Board was equally adamant that he had no such power.

By the summer of 1831, Proctor was admitting to the Board that numbers were down and parents were taking boys away because of poor teaching, particularly in Maths. Parents were also complaining that the school concentrated far too much on Classics.

Proctor and the Board fell out further when they ruled he must pay for repairs to the Hall which had been damaged. Proctor refused: 'The College Hall may be thought of as a part of my House, as it is a place of thoroughfare for my boarders, but I can hardly be held responsible for any damage to it.'

The large reduction in the number of scholars meant tuition fees no longer matched outgoings on masters' salaries. The Board made it clear they held Proctor fully responsible for this untenable financial position. He promptly resigned by letter in October 1831, but worked out his contract as Principal until the end of the following summer term. It proved a highly damaging interval for the College, with the Governor, Lt Governor, Bailiff, Royal Court and Directors all embroiled in an acrimonious correspondence with Proctor about his conduct. When Proctor, before returning to England, asked for a testimonial, two senior Directors had their reasons for refusal placed on record: 'During the three years in which he filled the office of Principal, he failed to realise the expectations … which were founded on the testimonials produced by him.'

Within a short time of Proctor's arrival, the relationship between him and the Board began to deteriorate. Ominously, in the very week that his appointment was confirmed, the Directors were digesting a report which highlighted the unsteady state of College finances: 'We regret that the result is not more favourable but we trust it will have the good effect of showing the necessity of retrenchment. The present scale of expenditure cannot be continued without endangering the permanency of the institution.'

Nevertheless, the new College had hardly opened its doors when Proctor challenged his proposed salary. The Directors were later to regret their decision to increase it by 25 per cent. Apart from arguments over remuneration, Proctor also complained that his authority was undermined by not being allowed sufficient control over junior masters. He was adamant that he alone had the power to dismiss

Below left: Sir
John Lintorn
Simmons.

Below right:
Mt Begbie in the
Canadian Rockies.

Meanwhile, the search was on for someone who might bring greater stability to what, after all, was still a fledgling College. In the event, the Directors and Visitors looked no further than the College Vice-Principal of eight years' standing, the Revd William Davies.

Whatever Proctor's failings in administration, many of his pupils had followed distinguished careers, often overseas. George Carey (284) was a general in the New Zealand Wars and became Governor of Victoria, Australia, in 1866. George d'Arcy (309) was Governor of the Falkland Islands, and Field Marshal Sir John Lintorn Simmons (298) was Governor of Malta — at an Old Elizabethan dinner in 1895, Simmons put his career achievements down to 'being caned every day of my life at school'. Edmund Kennedy (348) was an explorer in Australia, after whom Mount Kennedy and a national park in Eastern Australia are named. MB Begbie (328) was British Columbia's first Chief Justice and also had a 'mount', in the Rockies, named after him. Begbie, knighted by Queen Victoria, was instrumental in defining laws which governed the gold rush in the 1860s.

Professor Sir Peter Le Page Renouf (389) was HM Inspector of Schools and Keeper of Egyptian Antiquities at the British Museum. Edward Somerset (211) combined a military and political career as an army general and MP: he represented Monmouth and West Gloucester. He also served as acting Governor of Gibraltar.

Sir Peter Le Page Renouf.

College congers

Edward Boys Ellman suggests a reason why Elizabethans were called 'College congers'. 'We all wore College caps; the sixth form with tassels, the others without them. The College cap was a dangerous missile, and I know of some most awkward accidents, such as a head cut open badly with them. These caps were commonly called "congers", being considered by the boys to resemble the shape of soup bowls, and conger soup being a common dish in Guernsey.'

College boys were still being called 'congers' in the 1950s. Replying to a correspondence in the *Guernsey Society* journal, the head of the Lower School, Major Caldwell, was surprised that the practice had survived the five years of German occupation and exile of the College to Derbyshire: 'I happened to be leaving the College by the Lower School door in Upland Road when the old cry, "College Congers!", was raised by boys from a town school. I have also heard the term whispered in buses where College boys were travelling in superior numbers.'

Two Oxford scholars had joined in the correspondence. FA Hayley (2708) had suggested the term came from a shortening of 'Colleger' to 'Coll'ger' and then 'some small wag substituted Conger'; AL Lee (2693) claimed it was down to 'a simple piece of alliteration' and BJ de G Mourant (2963) put forward the theory that it was a corruption of 'congés' – Guernsey boys at other schools were jealous that the College had longer holidays. A Jerseyman, CT Le Quesne, wrote that Victoria boys had also been 'congers'.

Doctor Blimber's Young Gentlemen as they appeared when enjoying themselves.

Dr Proctor returned to Sussex where he became headmaster of a school in the Kemptown area of Brighton. At that period, Charles Dickens stayed at the town's Bedford Hotel where he wrote chapters of *Dombey and Son*. It is claimed that Proctor was the model for one of the novel's main characters, the schoolmaster, Dr Blimber. The description of Dr Blimber by Dickens was: 'A portly gentleman in a suit of black, with strings at the knees, and stockings below them. He had a bald head, highly polished; a deep voice; and a chin so very double, that it was a wonder how he ever managed to shave into the creases.'

Portraits exist in the Le Marchant Room of every Principal of the College since 1824 with the exception of Proctor. We can only guess whether the description of Blimber was of Proctor himself.

Left: Dr Blimber with his charges in Charles Dickens' *Dombey and Son*.

Opposite: The Principal's front door, 1865.

WIDER HORIZONS

'Three or four of the oldest boarders were lying on the roof of the Hall in their dressing gowns and night caps, their feet in the gutter, each with a lighted candle, drinking glasses of grog and smoking cigars.'

THE FRENCH MASTER DESCRIBING THE LACK OF DISCIPLINE IN THE COLLEGE

*I*N THE EYES OF many Guernsey people, Elizabeth College had again become a damaged institution only seven years after its re-chartering. In England, however, it was beginning to be a different story, with the College increasingly gaining a sound reputation, undoubtedly owing to good public inspection reports by examiners from Oxford.

The senior College Director, Colonel TF de Havilland, delivered what he called a 'memorandum on the College system' in October 1832. While not exactly a visionary outlook, it did set the path for at least some academic reform and for many years remained the model on which College teaching was based. He called for a list of subjects to be taught throughout the whole school which would compare favourably with any such list today: Religion,

North aspect of the College – a lithograph in the Moss Print series by Thomas Compton, 1830.

View of St Peter Port, Guernsey, by Alfred Clint, oil on canvas, mid-19th century.

The view from London

The 1832 London-based *Quarterly Journal of Education* could not have been more gushing in its praise. It made the unusual point that although the school had cost the States £16,000 to set up with new buildings and staff, the island's economy was better off to the tune of £6,000 per annum because parents were not sending their sons away to much more expensive public schools in England. The College was flourishing 'to an unprecedented degree', said the journal, and the Oxford examiners concluded that 'young men from Elizabeth College had been found equal at least to accomplished scholars of the best English schools'.

The journal's generous seal of approval ended with an endorsement, which would hardly be judged a resounding compliment today, that education was on offer to the whole of Guernsey 'of a superior quality for those of the middling classes and of a sound useful description for the lower orders'. It would have pleased Principal William Davies, though, who had already begun to dedicate himself to the provision of a more general and liberal education, suitable for boys in the wider island community.

French, English Language and Literature, History, Geography, Maths and Natural Philosophy (Physics). Other general subjects on de Havilland's list, most of which have long since fallen by the wayside, were Rhetoric, Political Economy, Book-Keeping and Navigation. Interestingly, he suggested Classics should be available to all boys but not compulsory, a clear response to those parents who had complained of the slavish devotion to classical subjects under the first two Principals after the re-chartering.

De Havilland maintained his new system would produce scholars for the university and for professions in which 'Classics are deemed essential' but also qualify young men for the 'ordinary walks of society, especially in this island'. The Bailiff, Daniel de Lisle Brock, joined in the debate but was at pains to point out that whatever the College decided for itself in terms of curriculum was not the business of the Royal Court. That, however, did not stop him from articulating the Royal Court's opinion: 'Members believe they express the general sentiments of the inhabitants that the system of education at the College is exclusively too classical for the greater number. The future prosperity of the majority of the rising generation, and the interests of the College itself, urgently require that the system be enlarged.'

The Royal Court will have been satisfied by the examiners' report at the end of the 1834 summer term when they highlighted 'the success of the Principal who has developed the powers of the less quick as well as the cleverer boys'.

Major army school

The establishment of a Royal Military College at Sandhurst was the brainchild of Major-General John Gaspard Le Marchant, a member of the old-established Guernsey family which provided island Bailiffs almost continuously from 1728 until 1810 – there was a Bailiff Le Marchant as early as the reign of Edward III. General Le Marchant himself was sent to a school in Bath in the 1770s, Elizabeth College being judged by the family as an unfit place for their sons to be educated. However, many Le Marchants in later generations did attend the College: John Gaspard's grandson, General Gaspard Le Marchant Tupper (442), founded the Tupper Army Scholarship at the College in 1908 and was a power behind the formation of the cadet corps. The College developed a deserved reputation for providing a good grounding for aspiring army officers.

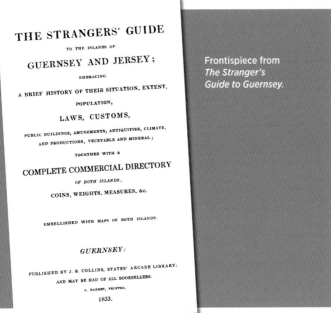

Frontispiece from *The Stranger's Guide to Guernsey.*

Published in the same year, *The Strangers' Guide to Guernsey* praised the College for its education which led a boy to 'acquire an adequate knowledge of commercial arithmetic and such proficiency in the French language as will fit him for future situations in active life'.

'Other studies', it added, 'in modern languages, military and civil architecture, drawing and surveying, afford many additional advantages, particularly if a scholar should afterwards be removed to either of the royal academies at Woolwich, Portsmouth or Sandhurst'.

Thomas Compton was the master in charge of Architecture, Surveying and Drawing. He was also the distinguished artist whose work remains in Guernsey's cultural consciousness in the form of the famous Moss Prints, which are still collectors' items in the island. The iconic lithograph of the College itself is Compton's work, as is another particularly sought-after print of Sark's Creux Harbour. When Compton left the College in 1825, the Directors gave him an outstanding testimonial: 'We are unanimous in our opinion that your abilities are of the first order, your assiduity in the discharge of your duties has been unremitting and we have heard, with considerable regret, of your intention to remove from the island.'

Science generally was beginning to play an increasingly important part in College life, both in and out of the classroom, although the modernisation of the curriculum was nowhere near fast enough for some reformers.

In 1837, the Lt Governor, General Sir James Douglas, attended a meeting of the Directors and proposed that 'for the instruction of the rising generation and gratification of every class of society in the island, it is very desirable that a library, a laboratory, a museum and other means of enabling competent persons to give lectures on scientific

Creux Harbour, Sark, one of the most popular of Thomas Compton's lithographs. (EP Cachemaille (1011) of Sark was a distinguished scholar and author who emigrated to New Zealand in 1894.)

subjects, be provided for the use of the College'. Sir James suggested he should give the first lecture and presented the College with 'an electrifying machine and an air pump for the use of subsequent lecturers to illustrate their subjects'. He tried to persuade the College to set up a department of civil engineering similar to one he had seen at a school in London. After lengthy discussions on the Lt Governor's recommendations, the College authorities decided a series of lectures should go ahead, but setting up a museum or a laboratory was unaffordable. Sir James's electrifying machine and air pump went unused and they were handed on to a more grateful Guernsey Mechanics Institution. Nonetheless, Principal Davies clearly thought he should be more positive about the teaching of Science and appointed a Professor of Natural Philosophy, George Bachhoffner, to the staff. The move was not exactly a seismic shift away from the old order, although, as Bachhoffner had just founded the London Polytechnic, he was certainly a man of the moment. Confirming the appointment to the Directors, Davies admitted that he expected Professor

Bachhoffner to be only 'an annual or at least an occasional visitor to the island'.

This was the beginning of the age of electricity. When Queen Victoria acceded to the throne in 1837, Michael Faraday had already invented the electric motor and gave some of the first Royal Institution's Christmas lectures for children of school age – the lectures survive to this day and are televised to a wide audience. These life-changing advances were the background to various attempts by staff and others to modernise the College curriculum, but even the most modest reforms were generally turned down. In 1843, a teacher of Phonography and Stenography (shorthand and typing) was on the staff list, although the Principal did not expect his services would be 'much required by our scholars'. An offer by a member of staff to introduce 'vocal music' classes fell on deaf ears; in contrast, the appointment of a master to teach German was regarded as highly successful.

However, despite the best efforts of some enlightened islanders, the College was still weighed down by the Classics.

Above: Portrait of the Revd William Davies from the Le Marchant Room Collection.

Right: Michael Faraday lecturing on the use of electricity.

A typical examiners' report in the 1840s contained nine paragraphs on achievements in Classics and theology, one on mathematics and nothing on any of the other subjects studied.

One of the biggest problems, as ever, was finance. Extra subjects meant extra teachers, but with no increase in the number of fee-payers on the roll, there was no additional income. The Directors, laughably, were seduced by a suggestion that they should appoint a 'Regius' Professor of Natural Philosophy, in other words they should ask the Queen herself to fund the position of a Science master. The resulting 'Humble Petition of the Directors of Elizabeth College to the Queen's Most Excellent Majesty' set out the pious reasons for the request:

'It is of the utmost importance to the inhabitants of Guernsey that this establishment should afford them every facility for the complete education of the youth of the island in the various branches of science as, from its geographical position, they are precluded from availing themselves of those opportunities in the Mother Country.'

Extracts from the Petition to Queen Victoria to fund a science Master in 1844, signed by the Bailiff and other senior islanders.

51

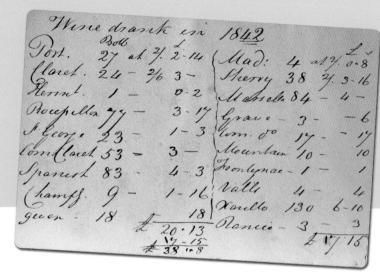

Above: Money may have been short, but the Principal's wine bill for 1842 was still substantial.

Left: Room 2, 1906.

There was reference to 'the limited income' of the College and the advantages of a scientific instruction which 'cannot fail to be evident to Your Majesty'. Unsurprisingly, the high-blown aspirations of the Directors fell at the first hurdle when the Home Secretary, Sir James Graham, agreed to lay the petition before Her Majesty but refused to advise her to accept it. It is unlikely that she ever had sight of it.

Paying for staff was no longer the sole financial concern. The maintenance of the grounds and building, only 15 years old, was also becoming a costly problem. Open drains running alongside the Vice-Principal's house were a health risk and in need of renovation. The Principal reported that cold classrooms were making the boys ill and 'the noise of the windows during the stormy seasons is obstructing conversation between master and pupil'. The College carpenter, Daniel Mollet, claimed the chimneys in rooms which had fires could not be swept as 'owing to their construction, the sweeping machine is totally inefficient'. The problem had been made worse, and costs increased, by a change of the law in England, and subsequently in Guernsey, which 'prohibited entirely the employment of climbing boys' to sweep chimneys. After complaints from the owners of

properties adjoining the College grounds, boundary walls also had to be rebuilt at the expense of the College.

Although the turbulence of the 1820s had given way to a period of relative calm, the storm clouds were gathering once again. Numbers at the College were on the decrease once more and William Davies, a much respected Vice-Principal and Principal for nearly a quarter of a century, stood accused of presiding over a failing institution.

The Directors set out their complaints in a long letter to Davies: 'You are doubtless not ignorant that dissatisfaction is felt with the present state of the College … you have received, as we understand, complaints of the inefficiency of masters … it is now common practice for parents to withdraw their children from the school and have them instructed by private masters.'

The French master, Mons Le Courtois, they alleged, refused to speak to the boys in the French language and also employed himself 'reading and writing things not connected with his business in school hours'. Le Courtois appeared to blame the unruliness of the boys for his shortcomings. He had witnessed a group in the library, 'drinking port and other liquors, and rolling the empty bottles up and down a picture which they were using as a table for their orgies'. One night he had discovered three or four of the oldest boarders lying on the roof of the Hall, 'in their dressing gowns and night caps, their feet in the gutter, each with a lighted candle, drinking glasses of grog and smoking cigars'. It seems Le Courtois felt powerless to do anything about the unruliness. It was not until much later that he was sacked.

The Directors were also damning of the conduct and discipline of the boys. Even in the College playground there was little supervision, they said. 'With reference to the use of wine and spirits, which we fear prevails, several boys have been observed from the adjoining houses to indulge in them to the great discredit to the institution.'

The Principal's reply was to rebut all the accusations and then thank the Directors for 'the delicate way in which their suggestions were made'. Only days later, they received a further communication from the Principal: 'Circumstances of a family nature have rendered desirable my residence in England and, in consequence, I am desirous of resigning the office which I have held for so long and with so much pleasure.'

The circumstances surrounding the Davies resignation were nothing compared with the bitter war of words between the College and the Lt Governor which was to follow. It involved not only Her Majesty's Government at Westminster but Her Majesty the Queen herself.

College boys and others under the gas light outside the Porter's Lodge in 1865. Gas lighting had been installed in the Principal's rooms a decade earlier.

6

GENERAL OFFENSIVE

'The little College boys shouted for me and I spoke to them and got a holiday, for which I am much loved by the said boys.'

GENERAL WILLIAM NAPIER, ON HIS ARRIVAL AS LT GOVERNOR OF GUERNSEY

'The College, already sinking, will go to ruin. It will again become the contemptible, corrupt, useless institution it was.'

GENERAL NAPIER, AS HE APPROACHED THE END OF HIS TERM AS LT GOVERNOR

W HEN QUEEN VICTORIA and Prince Albert paid a so-called surprise visit to Guernsey on 24 August 1846, the Royal Yacht *Victoria and Albert* had anchored in the Little Russel the previous evening. The Queen was a prolific diarist and wrote of their arrival in St Peter Port:

> As we approached we were struck by the beauty of the Guernsey coast ... the town of St Pierre is so very picturesque-looking, very high, narrow and bright-coloured houses built down to the edge of the sea, the Church and College being predominant buildings.

Alerted to the sudden arrival of Victoria and Albert, islanders flocked to the town piers and esplanade to catch a glimpse of the first ruling British monarch to visit the

Queen Victoria and Prince Albert arrive in Guernsey – from a watercolour by the College drawing master, Paul Naftel, now in the Royal Collection at Windsor Castle.

General Napier.

island. It was a clear Sunday evening and as darkness fell, houses were lit with candles along the esplanade and all the way up through Hauteville. In her journal, the Queen wrote: 'We dined at eight and found, on going on deck, the whole town illuminated, which had a very pretty effect, and must have been done very quickly, for they had no idea of our coming.'

Charles Durand (1009), seven years old at the time, later recalled the historic visit: 'It was impossible to conceive the state of excitement that the island was thrown into, all business was suspended and every man, woman and child able to move was on foot at daybreak.'

Ordinary islanders were quite unaware of what had happened the previous evening when the Lt Governor, General William Napier, was ferried out to the royal yacht to greet the Queen on behalf of the island. The story is that she remained in her state cabin, refusing to meet Napier face to face; short-tempered and self-opinionated, the old soldier's dealings with the population had been causing considerable concern in Whitehall for some time. Arrangements for the Queen's landing at St Peter Port, the following morning, had to be conducted through her equerry, Lord Paget.

When the Queen and Prince Albert duly stepped ashore from what is now the Old Harbour, they were formally greeted by Napier, the Queen describing him in her journal as 'a very singular-looking old man, tall and thin, with an aquiline nose, piercing eyes, and white moustaches and hair'. The royal couple were taken by carriage up the High Street, Smith Street, past the College and up the Grange, cheered all the way with flowers strewn ahead of them. Queen's Road and Prince Albert Road were named to commemorate their visit.

The Queen had noted in her journal that the decision to visit Guernsey was on the spur of the moment and that, anchored off the Devon coast the day before, 'Albert thought we might perhaps manage to see one of the Channel Islands

… and so it was settled that we should go to Guernsey, which delighted me, as I had so long wished to see it'.

It has long been claimed, though, that the Home Secretary, Sir George Grey, had somehow engineered the Guernsey visit as a way of both placating island authorities and testing the inhabitants' loyalty to the crown. For three years prior to the Queen stepping ashore at St Peter Port, General Napier had not only been at loggerheads with the States, the Bailiff and Jurats of the Royal Court, but a petition had been sent to the Privy Council demanding the Lt Governor respect island rights and customs.

A memoir from Napier to Sir George Grey could not have been more fiercely critical of island government, 'in the hands of a clique of local families, chosen for life, irresponsible, ignorant, barely acknowledging the supremacy of the English Sovereign and seeking by all means to deny the power of the English Parliament'.

The petition against him, he said, was 'hawked about by persons paid so much a head for obtaining signatures … people in the poor house had their names put down without their knowledge. It is a tissue of falsehoods'. Napier was also scathing about local newspaper editors:

> The Editor of the *Star*, living here under a false name because he was cashiered for infamous conduct in some regiment, is just the unprincipled person such a background would lead men to expect. The Editor of the *Comet*, formerly a ship's carpenter, is an ignorant, violent savage, whose brutal conduct towards his family has driven his daughters to prostitution; the Editor of the *Gazette* is a man of notoriously profligate habits.

Queen Victoria was only in the island for a morning, but the visit was hugely popular and it gave birth to an unmistakable addition to the St Peter Port skyline alongside Elizabeth College, Victoria Tower.

Given Napier's dealings with island authorities, it was only a matter of time before this imperious and irascible former General would clash with Elizabeth College. As joint Visitor by Royal Charter, he was in a powerful position to make his views known. His association with the College started well enough: at his installation ceremony, he wrote to his wife, 'The little College boys shouted for me and I spoke to them and got a holiday, for which I am much loved by the said boys.'

Paul Naftel, RWS

For Paul Naftel, an aspiring Guernsey artist, the royal visit was a heaven-sent opportunity. He used his considerable talent to capture the arrival of the Queen and Prince Albert with an intricately detailed drawing, developing it later into a fine watercolour which he offered to Her Majesty. The Queen paid 25 guineas for the painting and it remains in the Royal Collection at Windsor Castle. For some time, Naftel had been popular as a private tutor on the island but the royal patronage confirmed his exceptional artistic talent and he was appointed Professor of Drawing at Elizabeth College, a post he held for 23 years.

In the summer of 1854, Naftel was honoured by Queen Victoria when she commissioned him to illustrate her visit to Alderney. When the watercolour was delivered, it was too large for the position the Queen had earmarked for it. Naftel agreed to paint a smaller version but asked whether he could charge 50 guineas instead of the agreed 30 as he'd had to paint two pictures. This was accepted by the Queen.

When Naftel left the College, it was to enhance his flourishing painting career by setting up a gallery in London. He is acknowledged as Guernsey's finest watercolourist and his works command high prices today in London salerooms.

Above: Paul Naftel's watercolour of the arrival of Queen Victoria in Alderney, 1854.

Below: One of Naftel's many celebrated coastal scenes, Moulin Huet, on Guernsey's south coast. The same coastline was the subject of paintings by Renoir.

Below: View over St
Peter Port, with Victoria
Tower on the right.

While he proceeded with his military reforms of the Guernsey Militia and attempts at political changes in the States, Napier had left the College to its own devices, but the bonhomie disappeared when the Directors needed to appoint a successor to Principal Davies. The mechanism for the appointment, laid down by the statutes, appeared to have been invalidated in 1835 when the position of Governor of the island was abolished as a sinecure but that of Lt Governor retained – most Governors had never come near the island. The statutes specifically required applications from candidates for Principal to be 'forwarded *through* the Lt Governor to the Governor'. As there was now no Governor, how should the Directors proceed?

Napier was quick to inform them that all the powers of Governor had been vested in the Lt Governor and they must act accordingly. The Directors were unhappy to be pushed around and dug in their heels. Deciding they should appoint Dr John Bromby as the new Principal, they addressed a letter to the Home Secretary, Sir George Grey, informing him of their choice. In accordance with island protocol, Napier was asked by the Board to channel the letter on to Grey. Government House was uncompromising: 'For the information of the Directors, His Excellency will proceed in the matter as he judges according to his powers. I am further directed by His Excellency to return the letter [written] to Sir George Grey as irregular.'

Right: Portrait of Dr John Bromby from the Le Marchant Room Collection.

Far right: Sir George Grey, Home Secretary in Palmerston's government.

An astonishing war of words between the parties followed, but there was no declared winner or loser when the Home Secretary simply confirmed that the Queen herself had approved the appointment of Dr Bromby as Principal.

Hitherto unpublished correspondence between the Home Secretary and General Napier, however, shows his extraordinary fury with the College authorities and the extent of the animosity between them. The College, he told Sir George Grey, had been shamefully mismanaged by the 'family knot' of Directors. 'If Bromby is not a firm man in sustaining his own authority, his learning and ability will go for nothing and the College will decay, even as it has been decaying for several years.'

A less adversarial General Napier later set out his personal view of what the status of the College should be. 'The College is not an island institution alone. It belongs to England as much as Guernsey and is, indeed, supported principally by English resources – the great body of scholars are English, Irish and Scotch. And the money applied from the *impôt* [on spirits] is drawn in great measure from the consumption of alcohol by English labourers.'

He was reiterating his view that the College was too important to be controlled by the Bailiff, the States and the Directors, all of whom, he thought, were engaged in a conspiracy against reform and against him in particular. Hostilities between Napier and the College flared up yet again when the new Principal, Dr Bromby, refused to renew the contracts of three under-masters, one of whom was the notorious Professor of French, Mons Le Courtois. Although Le Courtois had been at the College for more than 20 years, he had been found wanting on several previous occasions, parents frequently complaining of his violent and uncontrollable temper, and his record had been generally abysmal.

Napier demanded the masters be reappointed to the staff as Bromby had no right to dismiss them. Once again, the Home Secretary was brought into the bitter dispute and the Bailiff, an *ex-officio* Director, even travelled to London for crisis talks. The private correspondence between Napier and Sir George Grey again confirms, in graphic terms, how deeply contemptuous Napier was of the Board of College Directors. 'The cancer of the institution has been island intrigue and if measures are not taken to stop these intrigues, the College, already sinking, will go to ruin. It will again become the contemptible, corrupt, useless institution it was before Sir John Colborne revived it.'

Sir George Grey must surely by now have been tested to the limit by these domestic, petty squabbles between the Lt Governor of a small Channel Island and its public school. As a former Governor of South Australia, a former Prime Minister of New Zealand and now Britain's Home Secretary, he was used to dealing with more important issues of state. He decided to take no further part in the affair and asked the Queen to commission an enquiry by a Special Visitor, Dr Stephen Lushington, a distinguished judge, MP and parliamentary reformer.

Athletics

Athletics have occupied an important and permanent place in the College calendar since the 1850s, the first track and field events being held at L'Ancresse Common. The College sports champion is awarded the glittering Dobrée Belt, presented to the College in 1860 by Commissary-General John Saumarez Dobrée, a nephew of Admiral Lord de Saumarez and father of 836 and 1151. Dobrée had a distinguished record in the Peninsular War in the early years of the nineteenth century.

In its first eight years, the Dobrée belt was won by three of five Corfe brothers, sons of the Principal. No other family has come close to this except the Garlands, LRG and DMP (8267 and 8958), with two wins each for Lee and Dale. Dale was a member of the British Olympic squad at Beijing in 2008 and the Guernsey team for the Commonwealth Games on many occasions. He won gold medals in AAA and European Indoor Championships.

CF Grantham (1889), BA Hitchins (1987), WC Hinde (1961) and EC Mockler (2950) had the distinction of winning the Dobrée belt three years running. The appropriately named brothers, AE and HB Leapingwell (2625 and 2627), both won the belt.

CWPFR Dugmore (2675) represented Great Britain in the 1908 Olympics in the long jump and triple jump and was described in the 1915 *Sporting Life* as 'one of the best, if not actually the best, all-round athlete in England'. He was a familiar and striking figure (more than 2m tall) at sports events at the College Field in the 1940s and 1950s.

DMP Garland broke the island triple jump record three times between 1997 and 1998, adding nearly 1m to the previous record and setting it at 14.04m. MD Ashman (8566) set a new island pole vault record of 3.5m in 1998.

Above: **CWPFR Dugmore.**

Far left and left: **AE and HB Leapingwell.**

Right: **DMP Garland.**

Athletics team, 1948.

In 2010, at the age of 94, J Le Masurier (3764) was honoured with a place in the England Athletics Hall of Fame. 'Le Maz', as he was known by generations of British athletes, was principal AAA national coach for nearly two decades. His crowning glory was Mary Rand who, in the 1964 Olympics, won gold in the long jump with a world record, silver in the pentathlon and bronze in the 4 × 100m.

In addition to the Dobrée belt, there are some stunning athletics trophies. The John Carey Cup for senior cross-country was presented in 1868, the Giffard Cup for the house championship in 1925 and the Frank Carey trophy for house cross-country in 1928.

Above: 'Le Maz' was an accomplished athlete and coach.

Right: Athletics prize spoons from 1930s.

The Queen's Commission specifically appointed him 'to settle the matters in dispute between the Principal and under-masters' but also to suggest any necessary revision of the statutes. Within two months, Lushington had taken evidence from all the parties and quickly determined that Bromby was perfectly entitled to hire and fire under-masters.

The authoritarian General Napier, by now retired, had been overruled. The rights and wrongs of Napier's quarrels with the island authorities are still argued about. Guernsey's statesmen greatly resented interference with their system of government which, if not corrupt, was certainly out of tune with reform in England. At heart, Napier was a champion of the common man. The verdict of his biographer, Gladstone's Home Secretary, HA Bruce, was that the government at Westminster was relieved when Napier's term as Lt Governor ended, but the ordinary inhabitants of Guernsey had, to their cost, lost a powerful advocate for change.

Napier's quarrels with the College turned out to be of long-term benefit. Lushington's ruling confirmed powers of the Principal which, by common consent, were manifestly reasonable. They were incorporated into new College statutes which prevail, more or less, today. The Dean and Lt Governor were replaced by a single Visitor, from then on to be the Bishop of Winchester, acting at arm's length, as a one-man court of appeal.

Other significant changes were also taking place in the daily school routine under the direction of Dr Bromby. The Lower School was more tangibly separated from the Upper School 'because there generally exists a strong objection on the part of parents to send boys of eight to ten years of age to a school where they will have to mix freely with much older students'. The new 'Lower School playground' was constructed, bordering Upland Road, along with a new back gate and additional door to the College building.

Gas lighting came to the College in 1855. Dr Bromby's apartments were to be fitted with gas pendants, 'not including the chandeliers', at a cost of £23.10s, but it took another decade for gas to be introduced into the boys' dormitories, at a cost of £7.3s.9d.

Bromby decided on a new form of punishment. 'I much prefer a milder to a severe form of punishment and have always found a short confinement during school hours most effective,' he said, asking for the window recesses in the upper gallery of the College to be converted into 'lock-ups'.

One of the lock-ups where boys engraved their school numbers in the wooden panelling.

A new word entered the College lexicon. The infamous 'lock-ups' were installed in the north-facing top floor of the main building. The word, if not the punishment itself, remained in use for more than a century. It wasn't exactly the short confinement that Bromby suggested. He promised it wouldn't exceed three or four hours, but was better than corporal punishment as 'it is a wide known fact that flogging in many cases can only add a racy stimulant to mischief'.

'Wilson', the legendary College ghost which stalks the upper corridors, is based on the story of a boy being supposedly locked up and forgotten for such a long time that he died of starvation. A real and more mundane story survives in an account written by Charles Durand (1009). 'A cousin of mine, Charles Dobrée, was locked up and the porter was told to let him out at five o'clock. The porter, Nicholson, was a Peninsular War veteran, getting very old, and forgot about him. At nine o'clock that evening, de Vic Tupper, walking along Upland Road, heard amazing shrieks and howls and looking up saw a figure waving its arms about. He ran to the porter to ask if anyone was in the lockups. Old Nicholson seized his keys and cried, "It's Master Dobrée!"' The porter was retired soon afterwards when, apparently, his memory had gone altogether.

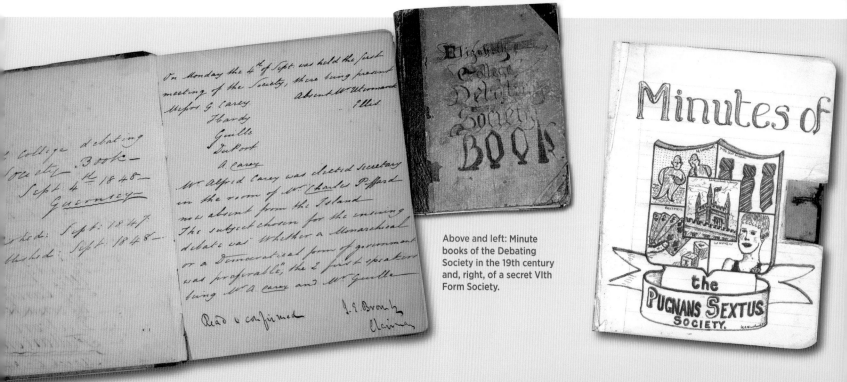

Above and left: Minute books of the Debating Society in the 19th century and, right, of a secret VIth Form Society.

Hugh Childers

HCE Childers was regarded mainly as a private pupil of the Principal. After attending both Oxford and Cambridge, Childers decided on a career in Australia and emigrated to Victoria. He was a member of the government of Victoria and became the University of Melbourne's first Vice-Chancellor.

In 1860 he entered the British Parliament as the Liberal member for Pontefract, and served in Palmerston's government. He was Secretary of State for War and then Chancellor of the Exchequer in 1882. He tried to resolve a budget shortfall by increasing alcohol duty and income tax, but his budget was rejected by Parliament and the government forced out of office. Later he was Home Secretary in Gladstone's short-lived ministry of 1886. Towards the end of his ministerial career 'HCE' Childers was notable for his girth, and so acquired the nickname 'Here Comes Everybody'. The town of Childers in Queensland is named after him.

Gaslights in Room 6.

In March 1851, the College suffered an appalling tragedy when one of the Principal's four sons, Johnny Bromby, was found dead. Boys had often played with and swung from the window ropes in the boarders' room, and the 11-year-old had tangled himself up in the ropes and accidentally hanged himself. A maid had found him, rushed to tell his father, and it was Dr Bromby who had to cut down his own son. Charles Durand wrote: 'A cloud fell over the whole school for he was very much loved and all of us went to his funeral. He is buried in Candie cemetery … we all subscribed to the beautifully carved monument'.

The remaining three years of Bromby's time at the College saw roll numbers again declining – 57 in the Upper School and 17 in the Lower School by the summer of 1854 – the Directors doubtless realising that Bromby's personal tragedy had taken its toll and the College was losing direction. Bromby resigned, emigrated to Australia and had a second, distinguished career as head of Melbourne Grammar School. Not least on account of his powers of oratory, Bromby had a huge influence on Alfred Deakin, one of his pupils. Three times Australia's Prime Minister, Deakin played a prominent role in establishing the federation of the Commonwealth of Australia. Bromby was also responsible for helping to create Australian Rules Football and the very first match was between Melbourne Grammar and their rivals in the city, St Kilda, in 1858.

Bromby's decision to go to Melbourne had undoubtedly been motivated by the presence there of one of his former Guernsey pupils, HCE Childers (958), who was the driving force behind the creation of Melbourne University. Bromby was the university's first Warden and was directly responsible for the admission of women.

John Bromby had left behind a Vice-Principal in Guernsey, the Rev Arthur Corfe, whose credentials were such that, in 1855, he was immediately promoted Principal. It all started smoothly enough …

Johnny Bromby's ornate grave in Candie cemetery.

ACADEMIC CONFUSION

'We are not aware that the College has sent to the universities a single distinguished scholar in the last twelve years.'

THE DIRECTORS REFUTING PRINCIPAL CORFE'S GLOWING REPORTS OF PROGRESS

HE COLLEGE HAD already acquired a good reputation for preparing boys for careers in the armed forces when the Revd Arthur Corfe took over as Principal in 1855. In spite of the continuous wrangling over funding and the difficulties of attracting and retaining suitable masters, the College was also slowly gaining more credibility in the academic world – Dr Bromby could point to several Open Scholarships to Oxford and Cambridge during his stay in Guernsey and he bequeathed some outstanding pupils to his successor. Bromby's leaving testimonial from the Directors included a list of some of the boys who had recently left school 'as an evidence of his ability and success as a teacher'. Du Port, Hardy, Walker and Carey,

Staff on the College steps, 1866. From left to right: Thomas Steadman Aldis, Maths master; the Revd Joseph Dobell, Classics; Mons Paul Stapfer, French; the Revd Arthur Thomas Corfe, Principal; Dr Johann Ely, German; Thomas Beesley, Commercial & Engineering; the Revd John Oates, Vice-Principal (later Principal).

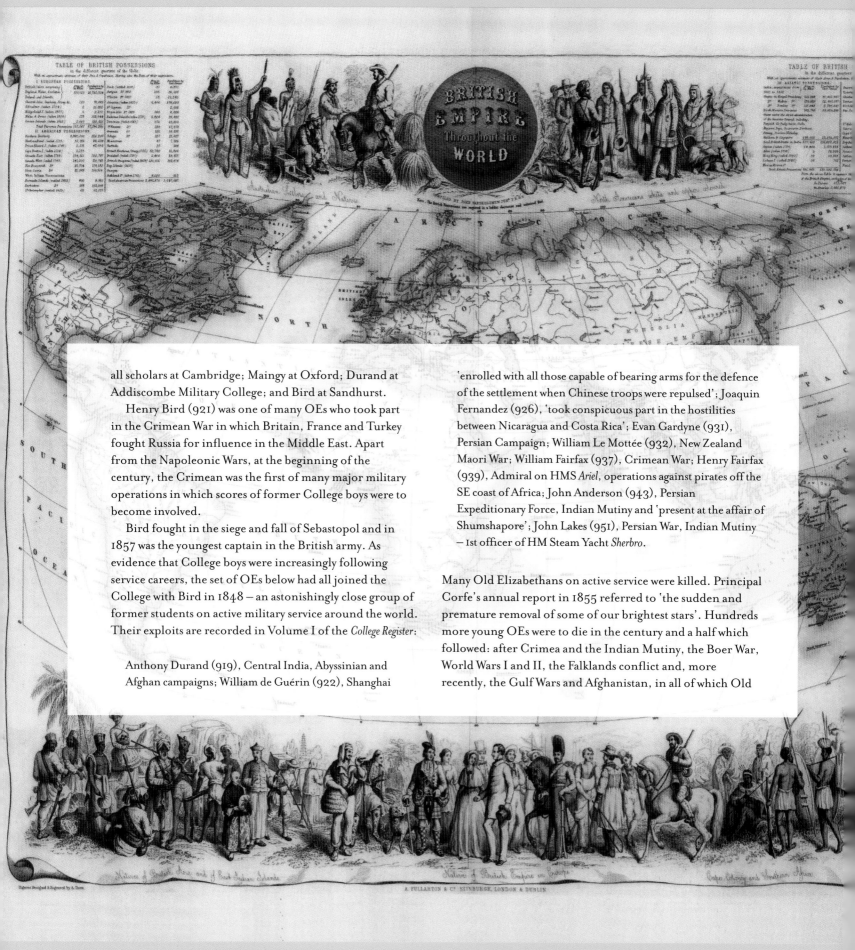

all scholars at Cambridge; Maingy at Oxford; Durand at Addiscombe Military College; and Bird at Sandhurst.

Henry Bird (921) was one of many OEs who took part in the Crimean War in which Britain, France and Turkey fought Russia for influence in the Middle East. Apart from the Napoleonic Wars, at the beginning of the century, the Crimean was the first of many major military operations in which scores of former College boys were to become involved.

Bird fought in the siege and fall of Sebastopol and in 1857 was the youngest captain in the British army. As evidence that College boys were increasingly following service careers, the set of OEs below had all joined the College with Bird in 1848 – an astonishingly close group of former students on active military service around the world. Their exploits are recorded in Volume I of the *College Register*:

Anthony Durand (919), Central India, Abyssinian and Afghan campaigns; William de Guérin (922), Shanghai

'enrolled with all those capable of bearing arms for the defence of the settlement when Chinese troops were repulsed'; Joaquin Fernandez (926), 'took conspicuous part in the hostilities between Nicaragua and Costa Rica'; Evan Gardyne (931), Persian Campaign; William Le Mottée (932), New Zealand Maori War; William Fairfax (937), Crimean War; Henry Fairfax (939), Admiral on HMS *Ariel*, operations against pirates off the SE coast of Africa; John Anderson (943), Persian Expeditionary Force, Indian Mutiny and 'present at the affair of Shumshapore'; John Lakes (951), Persian War, Indian Mutiny – 1st officer of HM Steam Yacht *Sherbro*.

Many Old Elizabethans on active service were killed. Principal Corfe's annual report in 1855 referred to 'the sudden and premature removal of some of our brightest stars'. Hundreds more young OEs were to die in the century and a half which followed: after Crimea and the Indian Mutiny, the Boer War, World Wars I and II, the Falklands conflict and, more recently, the Gulf Wars and Afghanistan, in all of which Old

Right: One of the earliest photographs of pupils, 1866.

Inset: Certificate of Merit, 1873.

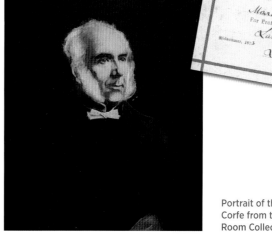

Portrait of the Revd Arthur Corfe from the Le Marchant Room Collection.

Elizabethans distinguished themselves. No fewer than four Victoria Crosses have been awarded to OEs.

The College in the mid-1850s appeared to be settling down after the previous periods of upheaval. In 1856, Principal Corfe expressed his extreme delight with 'the uniform and good conduct of the pupils on all occasions. Not a single complaint has reached me during the year of any moral delinquency'. Numbers at the College were rising from 67, when Corfe was appointed, to 150 three years later – and academic honours, he claimed, were on the increase. 'The university distinctions gained by the students of Elizabeth College are, to say the least, equal to those of any year in the annals of our institution', reported Corfe in 1857. Three open scholarships to Oxford had been obtained by his brightest pupils, JR Magrath (905), HA Giffard (906) and EP Cachemaille (1011), a native of Sark.

The euphoria over these hugely impressive results began to pale as numbers generally at the school were again on the decrease. Discipline in the Lower School once more became the subject of much criticism from parents and islanders. The Directors were now coming to the dismal conclusion that the reassurances about progress in the school in Principal Corfe's annual reports were fictional. The Board accused him of hanging on the coat-tails of his predecessor, Dr Bromby, and after yet another report of 'excellent progress' at the College in 1866, the Directors had had quite enough: 'The Board are unable to take that flattering view of the general state of the College which your report adopts … with the exception of two or three students, whose success must be attributed to the former Principal, they are not aware that the College has sent to the universities a single distinguished scholar in the last twelve years.'

Corfe had also been guilty of dismissing masters without any reference to the Directors and they complained that parents 'of the highest standing in this island' were removing their sons from the College to send them to English schools. Corfe had also ignored a demand from the Board to set up examinations in English, French and other subjects for boys in the Lower School. Relations between him and the Board deteriorated even further when he refused to meet dissatisfied parents, one father of three sons at the College accusing College boys of repeated verbal abuse as he passed the school gates, 'hissing and swearing and calling me a s..t'.

Intriguingly, two outstanding scholars, both OEs, Dr John Magrath and Henry Giffard, QC, were appointed by Corfe to be the school's public examiners. Their report highlighted 'the unusual amount of intelligence and promise observable in various parts of the school'. The Principal noted in his own annual report his pleasure that two natives of Guernsey, entirely educated at Elizabeth College, had seen fit to assure him personally 'that our own standard of classical attainments is equal to that of the best English

Scholars of distinction

JR Magrath and HA Giffard, who coincidentally had consecutive school numbers, 905 and 906, were the best scholars of their generation. Magrath had a remarkable career at Oxford University and was connected with it for 74 years. He was elected President of the Oxford Union in 1861 and then filled various posts at The Queen's College – Bursar, Chaplain, Senior Proctor, Dean and then Provost for 56 years until he died aged 90 in 1930. He insisted on inserting 'The' in the official title of Queen's College to emphasise it was named after a particular Queen, Philippa, consort of Edward III. Magrath was Vice-Chancellor of the University from 1894–1898. He presided over the second OE Dinner in 1893.

His friend, Giffard, took a First in mathematics and a First in Classics at Oxford and held several senior law posts in London before becoming a QC. He returned to Guernsey where he was elected a Jurat of the Royal Court in 1899 and Bailiff in 1902. He was knighted in 1903.

Above: **Sir Henry Giffard in his Bailiff's robes.**

Top left: **Portrait of Dr John Magrath from The Queen's College, Oxford, dining room, and (left) relaxing in The Queen's College Gardens.**

schools'. Magrath and Giffard could not, surely, have connived in anything untoward, but it was soon suggested that the boys had been exceedingly well prepared for the 'unseen' questions they faced during the inspection.

The clash between Principal and Directors was head on: 'That you decline to act upon the recommendation of the Board is a subject of regret rather than surprise … we cannot but complain of the manner in which our suggestions are usually received by you. We feel our relations with you seriously embarrass us … the only course of action open to us is that indicated by the 47th statute' (i.e. dismissal).

Further damning complaints about prefects handing out wholly unreasonable punishments to junior boys, chaotic teaching by masters and general incompetence in the management of the entire school were all now adding up to a complete loss of confidence in Corfe. The Lt Governor, Major-General Charles Scott, said he was powerless to intervene and that if the Visitor, the Bishop of Winchester, Dr Charles Sumner, could be of no help, he would 'make application to Her Majesty's Government to do so'.

The Directors were further outraged when they were barred by the Principal from entering classrooms to assess how French was being taught 'in an institution founded on land given to the people of this island, in a building erected by the States, the masters paid from funds collected by the States'. In Corfe's last year, 1867, the Directors refused to attend Speech Day.

The Bishop arrived from Winchester to hear all sides. His solution was to 'promote' Corfe to the Rectorship of Stockton, a very small village in Wiltshire.

If the official record of Corfe's time at the College is one of constant animosity, the published reminiscences of one of his pupils, AC Andros (878), paint a quite different picture: 'I regarded Elizabeth College as a university, inferior in no respect to that of Oxford and Cambridge or any other in creation and so I have ever since regarded it. Similarly, I looked upon the Principal and the Vice-Principal as the most learned pundits of the age and to this day nothing shall ever convince me to the contrary. I and all my compatriots at the College had more useful learning hammered into us, and enjoyed less skylarking and tomfoolery in Mr Corfe's room than any other room in the College – and as long as I shall live I shall always regard Mr Corfe with the highest esteem and veneration, though largely mingled with awe.'

The pages of the *College Register* also undermine Corfe's detractors. There were countless entrants to Oxford and Cambridge during his tenure and a great many OEs subsequently had successful careers all over the world, including Corfe's own sons. Sir Henry Austin Lee (1405), for example, was a distinguished British diplomat, particularly well known for his work in Paris and New York, who worked with both Disraeli and the Marquess of Salisbury. Sir Austin was the tenant of Jethou from 1890

College cricket

1989	D. J. MARSHALL	in Jersey	115	NOT OUT
1989	S. B. R. MACKAY	-- Guernsey	100	NOT OUT
2005	J. A. J. NUSSBAUMER	~~ Guernsey	107	NOT OUT
2007	C. J. WHITWORTH	~~ Jersey	112	

George Bailey in the cricket team of 1868, standing far right.

It was under Principal Corfe, in 1862, that the first inter-insular cricket matches were held against Victoria College in Jersey. It was a fittingly equitable beginning to the series of blood matches that has been such a feature of sporting life in the islands ever since – Elizabeth won in Jersey and Victoria in Guernsey. One of the mainstays of the Elizabeth College XI was CC Corfe (1130), the second of the Principal's five sons, all of whom were at the College. Charles won a scholarship to Cambridge and had a formidable sporting record at the university. He emigrated to New Zealand, where he became headmaster of Christ Church College and was one of the figureheads

in the development of New Zealand cricket. He achieved almost legendary status in the country.

The captain of the College cricket XI in 1869/70 was GH Bailey (1634), who emigrated to Tasmania where he remains a cricketing hero. He was chosen to join the Australian national team on its first visit to England in 1878. The team beat an MCC side which included the formidable WG Grace.

College cricket faltered under Principal Oates and the Jersey matches were only re-established in the 1880s. The first century against Victoria was scored at the College Field in 1895 by LD Watling (2548). Other significant innings which appear on the honours board in the pavilion were by the brothers JV and CE Blad (3130 and 3131) in 1914, a partnership between RCN Roussel (4475) and CLC Fitzgerald (4451) in 1953, and the record of NK Howick (5923), who scored centuries in three consecutive years starting in 1969. JV Blad's 209 not out in Jersey still stands as the highest score on the board.

More recent notable achievements were the 793 runs scored by SBR Mackay (7668) in the 1989 season. There were three days to remember in 2008 – the day after winning the OE match, the first XI beat Victoria by four wickets and the following day saw off the MCC by three wickets. A big-hitter for the College in all three matches was TJ Ravenscroft (9369), who, during the match, scored 38 from one over. Two years later, he left the College to join Hampshire Cricket Club on a professional contract. One College master in particular, Jack Reddish, was inspirational on the cricket field and served the College for several decades in the mid-twentieth century.

Tim Ravenscroft.

until 1918. His brother, George Lee (1418), was ordained and returned to Guernsey, later becoming Dean, and is acknowledged as one of Guernsey's finest antiquarians. He was also a long-serving College Director.

When Corfe went, it was the end of another difficult episode for the College. The Vice-Principal, the Rev John Oates, was promoted to Principal and Guernsey hoped it had seen the last of turbulent priests running its public school.

Old Elizabethan VCs

For a school the size of Elizabeth College, to have four of its former pupils awarded the Victoria Cross for conspicuous bravery in the face of the enemy is a remarkable record. The widely differing countries where they won their VCs – India, China, South Africa and North Africa – underline the extent to which Old Elizabethans travelled around the world to serve their sovereign and their country. There is no higher award for gallantry than the Victoria Cross and it supersedes all other British decorations.

Home met his death when he accepted the further task of blowing up a fortress. After exploding several mines, he went to deal with the last. Thinking the fuse had gone out he went to relight it and the mine exploded, killing him. He was awarded the VC posthumously, just a year after Queen Victoria had introduced the medal.

Surgeon John McCrea (1545) was born in Madras and after eight years at the College, he went to Guy's in London to train as a doctor. In 1878, he volunteered for the Zulu War and was appointed Civil Surgeon to HM Forces in Cape Town. In 1879, the Cape Colonial government grew concerned at the amount of gun-running on the Basuto border and when it tried to disarm the Basutos, they rebelled. Fighting then took place on seven fronts, with the main engagements around Mafeteng. In one fierce battle at Tweefontein, when 16 militia members were killed, Surgeon McCrea, under heavy fire, helped carry a wounded yeoman to the shelter of a large antheap. While on his way to fetch a stretcher, McCrea was shot through the chest. He plugged his own wound with gauze and carried on attending the wounded. The action lasted for five hours, mostly in pouring rain, before the Basutos were driven back.

In 1881, at the presentation ceremony of the VC in King William's Town, Brig General Charles Clarke said: 'The Colonial forces and the medical profession should be proud of having in their ranks a gentleman capable of such heroism and devotion to duty.'

The painting of McCrea, below, commissioned by the Royal Army Medical Corps, is of the scene where he won his VC. It now hangs in the former army staff college at Camberley in Surrey where the RAMC has its headquarters.

Lieutenant Duncan Home (665) won his VC during the Indian Mutiny in 1857. The walled city of Delhi became the focus of the mutiny by soldiers of the Bengal army who no longer accepted British authority. The conflict was later chronicled by historians as the first Indian war of independence.

Home, an engineer, was given the desperate responsibility of blowing up the Kashmiri Gate to force an entry into Delhi. WHG Kingston's *Memoir of Duncan Charles Home* gives the following account of the action by Home and his section: 'Shot, shell and bullets were whistling thickly around them but through the terrific storm they marched on unhurt. They reached the deep ditch where the drawbridge across had almost been destroyed. It was not a moment for hesitation. Duncan Home sprang on ... he and his companions rushed across the bridge in the face of deadly fire and boldly lodged their powder against the gate ... the enemy kept its murderous fire on them. The gateway was carried and Britain's avenging hosts poured into the blood-stained city.'

Right: Portrait of General Halliday in the Royal Marines Museum, Portsmouth.

Far right: Major Le Patourel, his medals, Guernsey Post Office stamps issued in his honour, and, below, the Terence Cuneo painting of his exploits in the Royal Hampshire Regiment Trust's museum in Winchester.

General Sir Lewis Halliday (2237) won his VC for bravery in China. In 1898, groups of peasants in northern China began to band together into a secret society, called the 'Boxers', intent on destroying the Ch'ing dynasty which had ruled China for more than 250 years. They wanted, too, to rid China of foreigners. The Boxer Rebellion moved into the capital of Peking (Beijing) and an international force, including British soldiers, was sent to subdue the rebels.

When the Boxers attacked the British legation in Peking, Captain Lewis Halliday led a party of 20 Royal Marines and fought a desperate hand-to-hand battle. Before he could use his own revolver, he was shot through the left shoulder, the bullet carrying away part of his lung. In spite of his serious injuries, Halliday fought on, killing three of the enemy. Telling his men to 'carry on and not mind me', Halliday walked back unaided to a hospital three miles away.

Halliday rose to the rank of General and was knighted in 1930. From 1933 until 1946, he was Gentleman Usher to the Sword of State, responsible for bearing the sword before the monarch at ceremonial occasions such as the State Opening of Parliament.

Brigadier Harry Le Patourel (3811) left the College in 1934 for a job in banking, but decided he would prefer a career in the army and joined the Hampshire Regiment in 1938. In World War II, the second battalion of the regiment was involved in the battle of Tebourba, a town 20 miles west of Tunis, in North Africa. Le Patourel led a party of four men in a daring raid on a machine gun position occupied by the enemy on higher ground. The party came under sustained and heavy enemy fire, although it had destroyed several machine gun posts. When all of his fellow combatants had been killed or wounded, Le Patourel went forward alone with pistol and grenades to attack the remaining enemy posts at close quarters.

Le Patourel accompanied the Home Secretary, Herbert Morrison, on a visit to Guernsey shortly after the liberation of the island in 1945. Morrison reported back to the Cabinet that 'as can be imagined, Le Patourel's reception was tumultuous'.

1802

Victor Hu

188

VICTOR HUGO
EN VILLE

'Unlike their French counterparts, the boys of Elizabeth College become more pleasant as they get older. Allowing them some independence changes them from children to responsible young men.'

<small>PAUL STAPFER, FRENCH MASTER AND FRIEND OF VICTOR HUGO</small>

WHEN JOHN OATES took over as Principal, Guernsey had for several years been host to Victor Hugo, arguably France's greatest writer. A political exile from his mother country, Hugo had also been expelled from Jersey for his anti-royalist views and arrived in Guernsey as a refugee. The *Gazette de Guernesey* was overjoyed that Hugo had acquired a property in Hauteville, 'proof that the great poet is happy in our midst and intends to remain in Guernsey'.

One man who acknowledged his pre-eminence more than most was an awestruck French master at the College, Paul Stapfer, who also lived in Hauteville. In the preface to his *Causeries Guernesiaises*, Stapfer describes going to see Hugo at Hauteville House, expecting to meet an ill-tempered,

Victor Hugo's statue in Candie Gardens, unveiled 7 July 1914.

Above: Paul Stapfer in later life and a dedication to him from Hugo.

Below: Covers of two Stapfer books, one dedicated to Hugo.

The dining room at Hauteville House where Paul Stapfer was a regular guest. Paul Stapfer left the College for an academic life in Paris and Bordeaux.

self-centred demi-God. Instead, he discovered an extremely polite, convivial 'gentilhomme', an elegant man full of old-world charm. Hugo was gracious enough to tell Stapfer that he considered it an 'honour to have him as a companion'. The two became firm friends and would meet often to discuss the merits of both French and English literature. At dinner in Hauteville, the innermost circle was Hugo, his two sons, his fellow exile and journalist, Hennet de Kesler, Stapfer and the editor of the *Gazette de Guernesey*, Henri Marquand.

Stapfer was astonished that, with a few exceptions (notably the Bailiff, Sir Peter Stafford Carey, and his daughter), the people of Guernsey treated one of the world's greatest literary figures with complete disdain. The rest of Stapfer's academic life was coloured by his contact with Hugo in Guernsey: in France he became a respected literary critic and authority on Hugo's works. Although he regarded many of his senior students at the College as friends and thoroughly enjoyed his time as French master, he hated the humdrum business of correcting their work. He was at a loss to understand why his English teaching colleagues much preferred the cane rather than detention for errant boys.

In *Victor Hugo à Guernesey: Souvenirs Personnels*, Stapfer recalls walking through St Peter Port one evening, returning to the College, and bumping into Hugo. 'I want you to meet Madame Hugo — she's coming from Paris', he said, inviting Stapfer to dinner on the following Saturday. Stapfer thanked him, explained he was suffering from severe headaches and was unsure whether he'd be better by the weekend. 'Bah! D'ici à samedi vous avez le temps de devenir amoureux. Vous savez que c'est la remède souverain contre les maux de tête? (Loosely translated: 'Good heavens, man! Go and have sex with someone, for headaches it's the best cure there is.') When Stapfer went on holiday to Paris, Hugo urged him to 'yield entirely to the charms of Parisian women'.

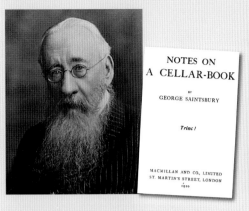

Above: George Saintsbury, Classics master, who became a world authority on English Literature and a renowned wine expert.

Left: Portrait of the Revd John Oates from the Le Marchant Room Collection.

Below: The artist, Peter Le Lievre, subject of a commemorative Guernsey stamp issue and the blue plaque on his house in Hauteville.

Le Marchant Library, 1924.

One of Stapfer's colleagues on the College staff was George Saintsbury, the senior Classics master, who was later to become a renowned wine writer and, as a professor at Edinburgh University, the foremost literary critic of his day. Saintsbury, too, was a fervent Hugo admirer and regretted never having had the privilege of actually meeting him. In his celebrated *Notes on a Cellar Book*, he describes almost, but not quite, engaging him in conversation in a St Peter Port wine shop, 'a queer emporium of furniture, curiosities, second-hand books and heaven knows what else – it was the only place where I ever heard Victor Hugo speak'. For some unaccountable reason, Saintsbury felt too reticent to introduce himself to the great man.

In January 1868, a troupe of actors arrived in the island to perform Hugo's controversial play, *Hernani*. Keen that it should be well received, Stapfer helped to organise an appreciative audience and recruited College boys to act as 'claqueurs' and 'bisseurs', friends planted in the audience to promote applause and cries of 'encore'. Stapfer named two of the boys as Freddy de Sausmarez and Edward Ozanne (later, Sir Edward, Bailiff of Guernsey). At the end of the play, one of the boys shouted, 'Three Cheers for Victor Hugo' (in English), acknowledged gratefully in the theatre by the playwright himself.

Along with Stapfer, one of Hugo's neighbours in Hauteville was Peter Le Lievre (80), a popular artist at the peak of his skill in the 1860s and 1870s and a contemporary of

Paul Naftel. Le Lievre was highly accomplished in other fields – he designed the two lighthouses at the end of the harbour piers in St Peter Port, influenced plans for the town market and at the Town Church, where he was churchwarden, the pattern of the organ pipes was his creation. He was chairman of the College Board of Directors for several years. A 'Blue Plaque' has been erected on the Hauteville house where he lived and worked just a few doors down from Hugo. His work was commemorated by a special Guernsey stamp issue in 1980.

A new emphasis on arts and literature was certainly developing at the College in the final decades of the 1800s, although nobody would have claimed the entire staff was now suddenly made up of a group of highbrow intellects. Oates, however, was taking care to appoint at least some commendably qualified academics. In his popular *Scrap Books*, Saintsbury wrote of his admiration of the forward-looking Oates whose writings 'had an excellent style and real critical facility. His sermons were never below a good average and sometimes much above it.'

Oates quickly established a school library in what is now the Le Marchant Room and paintings began to adorn the walls, not least one of the foundress herself, bequeathed to the College by Miss Leroy of Upland Road. A librarian was hired, to be paid £10 per annum, and a fund established to buy books which were not to be 'novels and light literature, the main object being to provide a good library of reference'.

Music was playing a greater part in College life, with concerts attracting audiences of around 500, not including College boys themselves. At a cost of £2 in 1870, the Principal ordered 'the printing of words of pieces to be sung at the musical recitation'. Demand for concert and 'speech night' tickets was such that a black market developed when boys began selling them to outsiders. To forestall this early entrepreneurial spirit, tickets intended for parents were sent out from the College by post and special messenger.

Old Cow Lane, St. Peter Port, by Peter Le Lievre, watercolour.

THE ILLUSTRATED LONDON NEWS.

No. 3129.—VOL. CXIV. SATURDAY, APRIL 8, 1899. SIXPENCE.

Above: The SS *Stella* by Henry Fowler, 10 September 1979; it was painted to commemorate the 75th Anniversary of the sinking of the *Stella* and copied from the original painting by JD Attwood.

Right: Newspaper account of the sinking of the *Stella*, 8 April 1899.

The College was also now beginning to sharpen up its image and appearance. The Directors had long discussions about what sort of ribbon should be worn on caps and hats, and decided in June 1871 on a striped blue/gold/blue band. The Directors' minutes record that a 'distinctive badge be adopted and that wearing it shall be obligatory for all the boys: the badge shall be a ribbon to be worn on the hat or cap, at all times except on a Sunday'. The rule later became more specific when the ribbon had to be worn 'all *round* the cap or hat instead of *on* the cap or hat as previously decided'. Principal Oates was soon relaying complaints to the Directors: 'It is not a pretty ribbon – secondly, it is liable to be imitated and counterfeited. One school has such a close imitation that I have considerable difficulty in determining whether a boy belongs to us or not! I would suggest a plain ribbon, either blue or scarlet, which should have the College arms worked on it. The prefects might have a different colour, e.g. scarlet, while the rest blue, or vice versa.'

In spite of his best efforts to improve both the administration and standing of the College, Oates soon found himself in the position so often occupied by his predecessors, having to explain why numbers on the roll were going down. He gave two main reasons: 'The gradual exodus of the English from the Channel Islands in consequence of the high cost of provisions and the strictness of discipline at the College which is distasteful to idle boys and is not appreciated by the parents.'

He also suggested other reasons for the waning popularity of the school. Masters were earning half the amount they would in England and yet the cost of living in Guernsey was the same. Doting mothers were a new problem: 'The loss of vessels between here and Southampton has frightened the mothers who are not only indisposed to let their children cross alone but also do not like to place 120 miles of sea between themselves and their children in case of illness.'

The Directors, however, had other ideas. They were concerned that the cane was being used indiscriminately by under-masters and this had become well known among prospective parents. Several complaints had been received from existing parents about the corporal punishment meted out by two masters in particular, Messrs Sheppard and Robinson. One letter, from General Herbert Abbott, pointed to something more than corrective punishment:

> The specific complaint I have to make against Mr Sheppard is, for having, this morning caned my son, No 1789, HWN Abbott, aged ten, inflicting twelve or fourteen cuts with the cane over both his shoulders and the exposed part of the calves of his legs, merely for some trifling error in a French lesson … I cannot allow my child to be beaten and demoralised by an ignorant and irascible master.

General Abbott asked to meet the Directors to discuss a practice which, he said, had led many parents not to send their children to the College 'in consequence of Mr Sheppard's obnoxious character as a master in the school'.

Boater ribbon, 1905–1931.

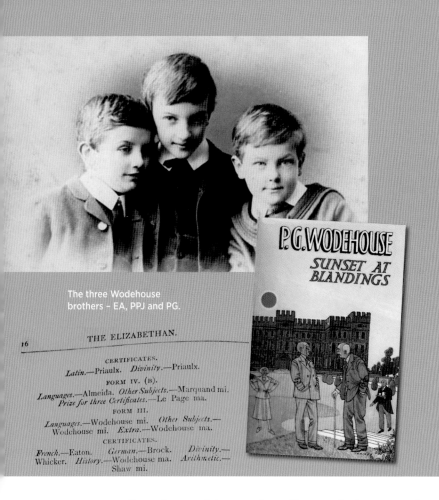

The three Wodehouse brothers – EA, PPJ and PG.

PG Wodehouse

PG (Pelham Grenville) Wodehouse (2618) was sent to the College in 1890, largely on account of his elder brother's weak chest – their parents thought the island climate would be beneficial to PPJ (Philip) Wodehouse (2617) and so the two boys were enrolled in 1890. PG or 'Plum' enjoyed his two years in Guernsey: 'A delightful place full of lovely bays ... our movements were never restricted and we roamed where we liked.' He hated the Channel crossings by mailboat, 'paddle-wheel steamers, like on the Mississippi, very small and rolling with every wave. It was hell to go back for the holidays at the end of the winter term. We would spend them with various aunts, some of whom were very formidable Victorian women'. The entry in the *College Register*, Volume II, simply states that PG 'followed a literary career ... contributor to *Punch* ... published many books'.

PPJ became a senior police officer in Hong Kong and was 'qualified in the Chinese, Hindustani and Punjabi languages'. The third Wodehouse brother, who entered the College in 1891, EA Wodehouse (2635), was a distinguished scholar. A double First at Oxford, he won the Newdigate Prize for English Verse and the Chancellor's Prize for English Essay. He was wounded in the Great War, but went on to become both a Professor of Philosophy and Professor of English.

Oates dismissed the complaint. 'I am perfectly convinced that any immediate change in the present system would be followed by a rapid deterioration of the intellectual and moral tone of the school.' Sheppard had caned a whole class for 'not doing a sum in the manner directed by him', but Oates maintained this was an offence for which caning was allowed in the printed regulations. Robinson was a new member of staff and had carried out six canings in as many weeks. The Principal defended him, suggesting that 'six canings are an unusually small number for a new master who has to establish a reputation for discipline'.

An all too familiar stand-off now existed between Oates and the Board. They wanted a new College bye-law restricting the use of the cane to the Principal and Vice-Principal, and called on Oates to appear before them. In accordance with the College statutes, 'the Board now requires your attendance' was the order handed down. The reply from Oates was: 'Respecting the discipline of the College, I must beg to decline any consultation thereon, as I maintain that it does not fall within the province of the Board of Directors to legislate on that subject.'

Once again the Bishop of Winchester as Visitor was asked to intervene. He ruled that under-masters were no longer to be allowed to inflict corporal punishment on the boys. Oates rounded on the Directors in a subsequent annual report.

Idleness is increasing at an appalling rate and we are all agreed that something must be done to check it. Now that the fear of the cane is withdrawn (except in very grave cases) one half of the boys do next to nothing – they have triumphed, they know it and are determined to enjoy the fruits of their victory.

In spite of their differences over corporal punishment, Oates seemed to enjoy the confidence of the College authorities in other respects. When he insisted that the prosperity of the College depended on three new facilities – a laboratory to cater for the new interest in Science, a gymnasium and a cricket ground – he received a friendly ear, although it took years for any definite plans to be drawn up.

An all-boy cast in *Much Ado About Nothing*, 1905.

The warehouse on the corner of the
Grange and Upland Road in 1850 which
became the Grange Club. A century
later it was acquired by the College.

The power games between Principal and Directors had
gone on now for decades, but they were completely
overshadowed by problems of funding. In 1876, the College
was in yet another crisis. It had to go cap in hand to the
States and its message was uncompromising: 'Such is the
present state of things that the States will have to decide
whether the College, which is of such benefit to the island,
is to have its efficiency kept up or whether it is to be allowed
to sink into a paltry, worthless, grammar school.' The
increase in the number of subjects taught, the additional
number of masters employed for modern subjects, boarders
more difficult to attract, 'timid mothers much frightened by
accidents which have befallen the mail ships', all
contributed to the hardship which the College now faced.

'The College cannot stand its ground unless the States
think fit to come to its aid.' In the event, the States voted to
subsidise the College with a grant of £400 per annum for
the following four years.

By the late 1870s, numbers on the rolls were beginning
to increase, but the question of academic standards became
an issue. The Principal wanted an entrance exam to the
College from the island's parish schools, but any such exam
would have reduced the number of boys at the school and
therefore the school's income. He deplored the low
standards in other island schools and the lack of culture in
the island as a whole.

> Every year it is more difficult to make boys work with a view
> to higher culture — culture, I mean, for its own sake, without
> reference to winning commissions at Woolwich or
> Sandhurst or posts in the Civil Service. At least one half of
> our present scholars seem to aspire no higher in literary
> attainments than they could reach in a well-conducted
> second grade school.

Oates was still blaming some of the low standards on the
withdrawal of the cane. The Directors were persuaded to ask
the Bishop of Winchester to relax the bye-law and,
surprisingly, he agreed. In the annual report of 1879, a

delighted Oates was able to describe the 'wholesome effect'
of the change on the junior classes and anticipated 'a marked
improvement in their work in a year or two as a result'.

Oates didn't miss any opportunity to press for a cricket
ground, a gymnasium and a fives court for the College.
'We shall never be able to put a stop to loafing, billiard
playing and smoking until some better provision is made
for healthy recreation and amusement. Boys prefer the
unwholesome atmosphere of the billiard room to the games
field. To be a member of the Grange Club is the height of a
boy's ambition.'

The gymnasium was eventually built after one of the
school's benefactors, Mrs Anthony Delacombe Maingay,
donated £1,000 towards its cost. Strenuous efforts by
College supporters and OEs raised enough money to go
ahead with the purchase of fields for a cricket ground off
King's Road. In 1886, levelling operations began and two
years later the first matches were being played on the
College Field. It signalled the end of cricket and rugby at
Cambridge Park and sports days at L'Ancresse.

John Oates had spent half his time at the College
campaigning for a cricket ground — within months of it
coming into use, he decided his work was done and
resigned. The vacancy was quickly advertised and interviews
arranged. The Revd William Penney made a deep
impression on the Directors — he was appointed on the day
of his interview in 1888 and he was just 27 years old.

The old gym.

9

PENNEY WISE

'The States should regard the claim of Elizabeth College for financial support as one of the most important items in the public expenditure of the island.'

PROFESSOR SIR MICHAEL SADLER, LEADING BRITISH EDUCATIONIST, 1912

'The right policy would seem to be the removal of the whole school and the erection of new and better buildings adjoining the King's Road playing fields.'

BOARD OF EDUCATION INSPECTION REPORT, 1920

WITHIN MONTHS OF taking over Elizabeth College, the young William Penney had put into effect a root-and-branch restructuring of the entire institution. After so many fits and starts and so many crises since the re-chartering, at long last here was a young man occupying the Principal's study with visionary ideas and the strength of purpose to carry them through.

Penney saw the faults of the place at once. Some subjects were badly taught while others, such as natural science, existed, if at all, in name only. Boys were 'lacking in *esprit de corps* and had little feel for the College itself'. The masters were characterised by 'unpunctuality and want of energy' and the building was badly in need of repair.

School assembly 1923. The Revd WC Penney is flanked by Messrs J Goodman and JV Thomas.

Portrait of the Revd William Penney from the Le Marchant Room Collection.

MAJORES MAJORA SONENT : MIHI PARVA LOCUTO

SUFFICIT IN VESTRAS SAEPE REDIRE MANUS.

VOL. I.—No. 1.   FEBRUARY 1, 1870.   PRICE, 1½d.

TO OUR READERS.

ON THE APPEARANCE of this, the first number of our Paper, we feel bound to offer a few words of explanation, in order to set forth as briefly as possible our motives, the object we have in view, and the results we hope to attain. Before however doing so, we wish to state, that though we by no means desire our undertaking to prove remunerative in a pecuniary point of view, yet we hope to avoid any absolute loss, which must accrue, unless our circulation be pretty extensive.

One of our chief motives for commencing this publication, is the fact that many of the English schools rejoice in the possession of some kind of periodical, and we do not wish to be thought behindhand in the world, because we happen to live in a somewhat out-

Penney's first annual review was able to point to the widespread remedial measures he had needed to take. An entire revision of the syllabus had already been introduced, masters' meetings were to be held twice a term and reports sent to parents every half term. Only the Principal and Vice-Principal would be allowed to use the cane. Chemistry lectures were to take place twice a week, with every class 'enjoying the privilege of an hour's practical work in Mr Nickolls' laboratory'. (For 15 years, Guernsey's public analyst, Mr J Nickolls, was almost singlehandedly responsible for College Science, teaching boys at his laboratory in St John Street, off the Grange.)

A carpentry group, musical society, choir, debating society and 'a useful reading society' were formed, and plans were in hand to start a natural history society. A fresh start

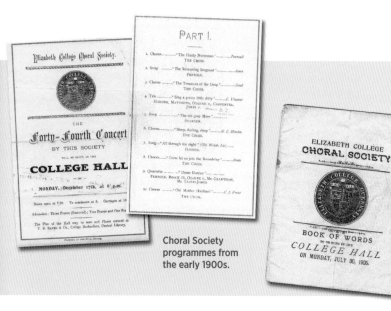

Choral Society programmes from the early 1900s.

would be made to publish *The Elizabethan* school magazine. Here, Penney was introducing the kind of activities which were already a normal part of life in English public schools and in which he had previously been involved at Cheltenham, Sherborne and Blundell's. The 'magic lantern', the predecessor of film, was also being used to illustrate lectures, many of them by the Principal himself. *The Elizabethan* noted in 1893 that Mr Nickolls had fitted blinds to the windows of the Hall and had also 'rigged up the screen so as to be available at ten minutes' notice: we are thus able to have Lantern lectures at the shortest notice at any hour of the day or night'.

All boys would play 'the national games' (rugby football and cricket) at least twice a week and 'the experiment of a match with Victoria College, Jersey' was to be tried. 'Nothing has been more marked than the improvement in games,' Penney reported, 'a steady average of from 80 to 100 boys on the field on all regular days for cricket and rugby football. The presentation of caps by various Gentlemen has largely contributed to this satisfactory state of things.'

College magazines

A number of attempts were made to publish school magazines and newspapers. *The College Times* published in 1853 was a handwritten bi-weekly journal which not only dealt with domestic College news but gave itself a much wider remit – in the editor's words, it contained 'the transactions of the week at home and abroad'. AC Andros (878) confessed that he and other writers indulged 'in the most scandalous and personal jokes at the expense of our schoolfellows – if one was fat, the Lord help him! If another was lean, we dragged him through a keyhole. If a third was short we dwarfed him to a pygmy'. The first journals to bear the title *The Elizabethan* were published in 1870 under the editorship of EP Thurstan (1648) and his brother, FW Thurstan (1649), who was later awarded the Chancellor's Prize for Verse at Cambridge. The magazines made irregular appearances and petered out altogether in the late 1870s.

Herbert Tourtel (2498) was the first editor of the reincarnated *Elizabethan* in 1889 and followed a career in journalism. He was the inspiration behind Rupert Bear, the *Daily Express* comic strip cartoon. As an assistant editor on the *Express*, he suggested that his wife, Mary, an established children's illustrator, should draw a children's strip, to rival others appearing in Fleet Street newspapers. With illustrations by Mary and captions by Herbert, 'The Adventures of a Little Lost Bear' appeared and Rupert subsequently became

one of the world's most famous cartoon characters. *The Elizabethan* has been published continuously ever since Tourtel's editorship, even in the war years, and its format and termly appearance remained virtually unchanged for more than a century. Today, *The Elizabethan* is a more lavish affair, in full colour, and is published annually. Other publications have come and gone, such as *The Rose,* a senior school literary pamphlet, and *The Rosette,* a junior school newspaper.

Left: *The College Times*, 25 June 1853.

Below: Rupert Bear, 1993.

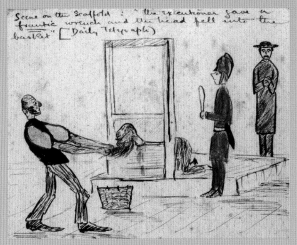

Staff caricatures.

Rugby football

It's not known exactly when the College started playing rugby football but the earliest photograph is of a XV in 1866 whose opposing teams would have been mainly drawn from the garrisons stationed in the island. In 1889, the first two inter-insular rugby football matches were played, Victoria and Elizabeth each recording home wins, 8–0 and 21–0 respectively. By then, though, interest in rugby in both islands was already on the wane and there was talk of changing to the Association Football code of rules. Both schools soldiered on for another ten years, but Elizabeth was the first to break away. In October 1900, *The Elizabethan* had bewailed the lack of team opposition. 'There is not a single Club in the island that can put a rugby XV in the field. Where are our matches to come from? The Secretary has been unable to issue a card of fixtures for the simple reason that there are none.' By 1901, the switch to Association was complete, but Victoria College was still wavering. This was particularly surprising considering Jersey had lost their final three rugby matches with Elizabeth, 65–0, 46–0 and 43–0. Association Football soon became popular in both islands and matches between the two schools began in 1903.

In the early 1900s, a group of OEs and one Jerseyman, all serving in the Siam (now Thailand) Constabulary, were so appalled that their schools had abandoned rugby that they commissioned a lavish trophy to help reignite interest. CH Forty (2518), as

Above: Rugby First XV, 1866.

Left: The Siam Cup.

The 1896 First XV with Cecil Forty, second from the right in the back row, next to Mr Arnold.

a high-ranking member of the royal household, was well known to the King of Siam, who gave permission for Siamese silver dollars to be melted down and used to make the trophy. He also instructed his own crown silversmith to carry out the work. The result is a magnificent work of art decorated with elephant heads and dancing girls. The five men stipulated that the Siam Cup was to be for competitions '... in any form of amateur sport except association football'.

Forty returned to Guernsey in 1920 and brought the trophy with him, only to discover that most other island teams had given up on the game. The cup was awarded in 1928 when a Guernsey garrison side, the 2nd Battalion the Queen's Own Royal West Kent Regiment, beat an island side. It is believed that the trophy was then used as a billiards challenge cup in Guernsey or a darts cup in Jersey. The first true inter-island rugby matches were re-started in 1935 when Guernsey RUFC won the trophy. During the war, the cup was hidden from the Germans and later emerged from someone's safe-keeping. Nobody knows where it was kept or by whom.

The Siam is the second oldest rugby trophy in existence, after the Calcutta Cup, and is competed for annually by the Jersey and Guernsey RFCs. It is of such historical value that it is held in safe-keeping by the Museum of Rugby at Twickenham and stands alongside the Calcutta and Cook Cups.

With Forty, the two other OEs involved in the creation of the Siam Cup were RD Bainbrigge (2707) and SP Groves (2767). Another, EW Trotter, was the father of two OEs.

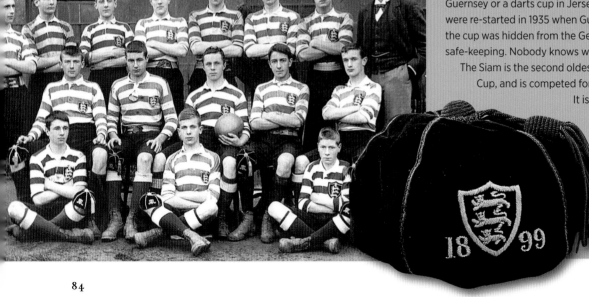

FOOTBALL FIXTURES, 1910.

DATE.	AGAINST.	GROUND.	GOALS. FOR.	GOALS. AGAINST.	RESULT.
Oct. 1	Rangers Athletic 1st XI.	College...	8	2	WON
5	United Banks' F.C.	College...	0	7	Lost.
6	Mr. F. W. Mourant's XI	College...	4	4	DRAWN
8	Pupil Teachers' F.C.	College...	7	7	DRAWN
12	2nd Batt. R.G.L.I.	Camp	SCRATCHED		
15	Belgraves' 2nd XI	College...	2	3	LOST
20	MASTERS Athletics 2nd XI	College...	2	3	WON
22	PUPIL TEACHERS F.C.				
27	United Banks' F.C.	College...	10	2	WON
29	Victoria College	Guernsey	1	4	LOST
Nov. 2	Royal Artillery	College...	3	4	LOST
5	NORTENERS F.C. Mr. F. W. Mourant's XI	College...	3	5	LOST
10	Athletics' 2nd XI	College...			LOST
12	Athletics' 1st XI	College...	4	4	DRAWN
16	Royal Artillery	College...	0		LOST
17	Rangers' 2nd XI	College...			WON
19	ATHLETIC ST MARTIN	College...	6	3	LOST
26	BELGRAVES	College...	5	2	WON
Dec. 3	Belgraves' 2nd XI	College...	3		WON
7	Victoria College	Jersey			

Elizabeth College 1910

Football Fixtures

E. C. LE PATOUREL (Captain).
N. H. LAINÉ (Secretary).

MATCHES PLAYED   WON   DRAWN   LOST

Above: Junior 1st XI, 1955.

Right: Guernsey celebrates 150 years of football, commemoratve stamp.

Above: Football 1st XI in Jersey, 1926.

Right: 1st XI, 2004.

Association football

Although some rugby has been reintroduced from time to time, football has continued to be the main winter team sport, with College teams represented successfully in many mainland league competitions.

Many of Guernsey's star players began their footballing careers on the College Field. The *Illustrated London News* in 1936 described JA Martel (3991) as an amateur forward 'than whom there are few better in England, let alone the Channel Islands'. DA Priestley (3717), Athletics Champion, member of the College 1st XI Football, Cricket and Hockey teams and Shooting VIII, played for the Corinthians in 1930. AM Hunter (4243), a King Charles I Scholar at Oxford, won his soccer blue in 1946 and joined the

College staff as a History master in 1948. Hunter was captain of the island's Muratti team on several occasions. CA Renouf (5266) was also Muratti captain and said to be 'the finest Guernsey footballer not to have turned professional'. Among other leading lights in Muratti teams have been JL Loveridge (5260), CP Gervaise-Brazier (5257), NA Le Page (5900) and CM Allen (8161). Allen played professionally in the North American Soccer League and the Major Indoor Soccer League. His son, RC Allen (9593), was named Guernsey FA Player of the Year 2009–2010.

In the 2004–2005 season, the College 1st XI won the Channel Islands League and reached the quarter finals in the first year of Guernsey's FA Cup.

Diners at the 150th OE Dinner in Guernsey in 2011. The OE Association, under the Presidency of MJS Eades (6529), had invited Dr Elizabeth Grantham (née Milnes) as Guest of Honour. There were so many applications for places that the function had to be relocated from the College Hall to St James.

The Hall, 1914.

In July 1891, the OE Association was formed after a set of rules had been drawn up at a meeting in the College library. It was one of the most significant moments in the history of the College.

A year later, a pavilion was built – a wooden structure, subsequently to be replaced by the present College Field pavilion – adding to the already large debt on the College Field. Bazaars, concerts and other money-raising ventures organised by an ever-flourishing OE Association finally wiped the debt off the College books in 1898, but it was a long haul.

The College corridors and the Hall were freshly painted, 'the effect being considered good by the vast majority of those consulted'. Penney had looked at the big picture. The state of the buildings, staff deficiencies and syllabus shortcomings had all now been addressed, but he had no intention of stopping there. He was also concerned about how the College presented itself to the outside community: 'A neat, inexpensive and

William Penney caricatured among the great and good of Guernsey.

uniform College cap has replaced the expensive badges and the motley variety of headgear to which they were attached.' The minutiae of the classroom did not escape his attention either: 'Steel pens and ordinary penholders have been introduced, instead of quills, thus effecting a considerable saving and also improving the writing.'

Penney promised to monitor the teaching ability of his staff by regularly sitting at the back of their classes. It was a brave promise – all of his subordinate masters were considerably older than he was – and they must have felt threatened.

He concluded his first report with this optimistic assertion: 'In moral tone, the boys compare favourably with those of any English public school. There is an almost total lack of ungentlemanly conduct even among the small boys.'

The early reforming zeal of the new Principal lost no momentum. In the boarding house when he arrived, there was one pupil: within a short time he had filled the house with up to 40 boarders, many, of course, from army families abroad. There was a regular flow of boys, at this time, from the far-flung cities of the British Empire – perhaps over-optimistically, parents stationed in the sub-tropics and elsewhere judged the Guernsey climate to be far less harsh than it was in England.

Although he now felt able to trumpet the calibre of his teaching staff, one master was still causing problems: George Metcalfe, the Vice-Principal. By the Principal's own admission 'a perfect gentleman', he was, nevertheless, unable to keep any order in class. In one case, four boys were sent to Penney to be caned 'for being concerned in an explosion in Mr Metcalfe's fireplace'. It took the creation of a new College bye-law making it compulsory for masters to retire at 60 to get rid of him. The Principal could at last describe his senior common room as staffed with 'one and all, thoroughly efficient men'.

Penney's personal workload was truly phenomenal by any standards. At the first OE Dinner, James Mourant (1207) proposed the *Floreat*. He had known three Principals: 'I don't know which to admire most, the discipline of Mr Corfe, the culture of Mr Oates, or the indomitable energy of Mr Penney. After a hard day's work in College, Mr Penney has been playing football with the boys, has given a lecture or preached a sermon and then wound up by conducting a two

hours practice of the Choral Society, I think he bids to go down in posterity as the "nimble Penney".'

James Mourant's son, Bernard (2963), later described a concert under the Penney baton:

Imagine some fifty boys and masters, the smaller boys in Eton suits, the grown-ups in tails, an orchestra which included Ladies' College girls and mistresses. How many of you can remember the scene at the end of the concert? One of the bigger trebles coming down to the front of the platform to sing the solo part of Auld Lang Syne, OEs, many of them come from the ends of the Empire on leave, leaving their seats to line the centre gangway and to join hands. Penney turns half left to conduct both choir and OEs as we sing the chorus with hands rising and falling in time to the music. It never failed to win an encore. Then God Save the Queen in full, for in those days we did not disdain to sing the second verse which has now fallen into such disrepute.

In 1893, the College staged an early 'Antiques Roadshow', described then as a fund-raising 'Loan Exhibition'. It attracted 'an avalanche of paintings, bronzes, furniture, porcelain, silver, Burmese and Indian gods, arms and

Loan Exhibition, 1893, and girls taking part in the associated 'theatricals'.

Combined Cadet Force

The Boer War led directly to the formation of the Officers' Training Corps (the CCF of today), the cost of which was mostly borne by some distinguished OEs. In 1905, the OTC received a royal inspection by the Duke of Connaught, Queen Victoria's third son. When the Royal Guernsey Militia was disbanded, the Cadets became the only uniformed military body in the island and ever since have provided guards of honour for visiting members of the royal family.

In 1956, Major George Curtis, three of the CCF's senior NCOs and the Bailiff, Sir Ambrose Sherwill, travelled to Munich to collect drums which had been taken from the College by German forces during the occupation. The drums had been looked after carefully by Herr Eduard Kohler, the last living Drum-Major of the Royal Bavarian army, who had won them in a music competition. Realising where they had come from, he organised their return. The hand-over ceremony included a colourful display by bands dressed in Bavarian costume. The CCF still performs the more traditional military and ceremonial duties, such as parades on Liberation Day, the Queen's Birthday and Remembrance Day.

In 1906, the College made its first appearance in the Ashburton Shield competition at Bisley.

The first full-bore match with Victoria was at the Grouville Range in Jersey in 1904, which Victoria won by 15 points. It was the beginning of the annual competition for the Haines Shield donated by Charles Haines (2877), who shot for the College in the 1900s.

Every single major trophy associated with the Ashburton has been won by the College, including the shield itself in 1989. In 1956, JL Ross (5028) won the main individual prize and MAJ Barber (10222) won the Schools Grand Aggregate in 2010. Many Elizabeth College marksmen have become 'Athelings' in the Great Britain cadet team to Canada, the first, EF Aubert (3527), in 1931.

Above: Ashburton Shield competition at Bisley, 1906, the first year the College competed; and the Ashburton Shield (inset).

Left: CMY Trotter is chaired off the Bisley ranges as Queen's Prizewinner in 1975.

Below: CCF, 1950s.

armour, fossils, birds and fishes long departed'. Lord de Saumarez lent paintings, the Bailiff contributed wax seals, there were pictures by Paul Naftel. It was a week-long extravaganza which included 'theatricals' with girls from the Ladies' College taking part. They were deemed worthy of a photograph on the College steps even though *The Elizabethan*'s critique of their performance suggested rather ungallantly that the second from the left, Miss C Hawtrey, 'was inaudible at times'.

As the end of the century approached, the efforts of the Principal were paying off handsomely. A playing field, a pavilion of sorts, academic achievements, a high flow of entrants to the service colleges, and what masters and others frequently referred to as *esprit de corps*, all were contributing to an increasingly settled status of the College.

The gaiety of the concerts and the theatricals – remember, the 1890s were the 'gay nineties' – was soon overshadowed by British involvement in the Boer War, 1899–1902. With so many boys going into the army at Sandhurst or Woolwich, it was inevitable that the clouds of war would soon begin to darken College life as news of casualties began to filter through. The Boer War was the start of half a century of such misery. The death of young Arthur Homan (2499) at the age of 19 brought an emotional address from the Principal. His words to the whole school in the College Hall would have been appropriate any number of times in later years. They remain as heart-rending a memorial as any to all our fallen Elizabethan heroes:

Today I have to speak of a young soldier, one of the three whom I remember sitting where you now sit, and who have lately given their lives for their Queen and country.

I hope you think it right that I should speak of Arthur Homan.

I will try to tell you what I remember and I knew him well. There is one place you will find no trace of him. Seven or eight years of school life, and not a single entry in the punishment book.

Ah ! – you may say, we know that kind of boy – too meek and mild to get into trouble and temptation.

Wait a moment.

The College VIII and OEs have distinguished themselves ever since in a way hardly matched by any other school. CMY Trotter (4180) won the Queen's Prize in 1975 and the St George's Vase at Bisley has gone to no fewer than three OEs, GT Martel (4496), MF Martel (4952) and FW Le Maitre (5019). Many other OEs have shot in the Olympic and Commonwealth Games.

I have mentioned the one place where you will not find him.

But you will find him —

On our Prize Lists, on the List for Woolwich, in the pictures of our College Theatricals, in the pictures of the House Elevens and Fifteens, in the pictures at the Pavilion.

I remember his dismay on entering the Boarding House to learn that he must not bathe throughout the winter. I remember a passion for combat with bigger boys, due, perhaps, to his Irish blood. I remember on the occasion of a Prince's wedding how he was disgusted at the apathy of Prefects and wrote to the Duke of York himself. And since he left us he has been perhaps the most devoted of all our younger Old Elizabethans. His very last letter shows his unflagging interest in the school.

No character?

It was as wholesome and hearty a young life as ever thundered up and down our stairs or made the heavens ring.

I am writing his last report and it is this: Blameless and harmless, a son of God without rebuke.

Guernsey melons, packed and ready for shipment.

Of the 133 OEs who served in the Boer War, nine were killed and many more injured. The honours list was two CBs, one CMG, six DSOs and seven Mentions in Despatches. We have paid tribute to our Old Elizabethan VCs on pages 70–71.

Meanwhile, at English public schools, significant developments were taking place in Science teaching. The need for a new approach to Science was made urgent when school inspectors threatened not to give the College the approval required by government departments and the Army in England. This would have been a disaster for the College, most of whose senior boys were in the Army Class. It led to the conversion of Old College into a fully equipped laboratory, a project paid for by subscribers and named after Edward Charles Ozanne (1458), a distinguished Guernsey educationist and horticulturalist. The States also gave a grant on condition the laboratory was made available to other island schools.

The establishment of the Ozanne Laboratory was part of a grand project to centralise scientific instruction for the whole island and especially for workers in such industries as farming and fruit growing: the soft fruit growing industry in the island, melons and tomatoes particularly, was then in its infancy.

The Ozanne building and its chemistry lab in 1920.

Flag-waving bureaucracy

One of the problems facing the College was excessive bureaucracy. The smallest issues took weeks to resolve. The entire Board of Directors climbed up to the Le Marchant room to discuss the proposed height of the College flagstaff, in the minutes thus: 'Resolved: the architect be asked whether a shortened flagstaff could not be affixed, with a topmast attached, which could be raised or lowered by the Porter when necessary and thus the expense of eight shillings and fourpence be saved on the occasions when the flag was hoisted.' Three army Colonels on the board, Durand, Yates and Glasse, were appointed to a sub-committee to 'consider further the question of a new flagstaff'. Months later, in March 1911, the board again climbed the stairs to examine the flagstaff, but postponed any decision because the flag wasn't flying. By October, the Board's secretary had visited the tower 'on Coronation Day when the flag was flying' and reported that the post was rotten and needed replacing because if shortened any more, the flag would no longer be visible from below.

Proficiency in Science was not pursued at the expense of more traditional means of learning. Under Penney, a large library of 12,000 books was amassed, partly with gifts of personal collections from Sir Edgar MacCulloch and, earlier, from Eleazar le Marchant, and partly by a modest, termly fee, levied on each boy. All the while, the College was finding it difficult to make ends meet. For some years, the Principal had used Speech Day as an opportunity for firm, if gentle, chastisement of the States for not supporting the College as they should. In 1912, he asked them 'to pat their patriotic bosoms and say they were as generous as the States in Jersey'.

Professor Sir Michael Sadler, a mainland specialist in the administration of education, was asked to look into education in Guernsey generally and the College in particular. He pulled no punches. The number of boys had

Jean Hugo

Jean Hugo (3182), Victor's great-grandson, was born in Paris in 1894 but from an early age lived in Guernsey, first at Hauteville House and then with his mother at Icart. If any one member of Victor Hugo's family inherited most of the great man's artistic talents, it was Jean. After Elizabeth College, he went to the Sorbonne in Paris. He returned to Guernsey with his father for the inauguration of Victor's statue in Candie Gardens in 1914. In the opening chapter of his *Le Regard de la Mémoire*, Jean describes how on 1 August that year he was collecting shells with his sister in Herm, with little or no idea that France would be at war with Germany two days later, a war that would change the face of the world. France and the United States both honoured Hugo's military service in World War I with the Croix de Guerre and the Distinguished Service Cross.

In the 1920s, Hugo was a prominent member of the Parisian glitterati, along with Picasso, Cocteau and Proust, and he gained wide recognition as a theatre designer, artist and writer. Of the College masters in 1908, Hugo had this to say: 'Mr Goodman, who taught Form I, smelled of beer; Mr Beuttler, the geography master, known as Mr Bottles, smelled of dried manure; Mr Lloyd Jones, pale as a button mushroom and who taught us Greek in the basement, didn't smell of anything. The long, clean-shaven face of Mr Andrews, with his upper lip projecting over irregular teeth, vacant eyes, baggy clothes, all made him look like a victim, strung up after a riot. The boys stepped up to his chair, insulted him, laughed in his face and even went as far as slapping him. The Principal, Penney, was a tall man: the vast expanse of his face, the colour of an egg shell, was marked by three black spots. He had a short moustache and his bushy eyebrows were always raised.'

Above: **Madame Georges Hugo and her son Jean, 1898 (oil on canvas).**

Above right: **Jean Hugo.**

been steadily decreasing and if it continued, 'the school cannot be carried on: this would be a disaster to Guernsey. The States should regard the claim of Elizabeth College for financial support as one of the most important items in the public expenditure of the island'.

There were further problems with the buildings. The Roman Cement on the main building was flaking off, the gym was sinking owing to poor foundations, and dry rot had developed, too. The College architect, Walter Quilter, had surveyed the gym: 'There appears not only to be a weakness in the foundations but also in the superstructure, doubtless partly due to bad design of the building and the weight of the roof. I do not consider the buildings to be safe.'

With the gym buttressed and the 'Repairs Account' showing a deficit, the Principal told a Speech Day audience that the States had 'spent money lavishly on Primary Education and should do as much for the College'. He urged the States to 'make a grant without any restrictions' for a new gymnasium, but it took more than a decade to happen.

The editorial of *The Elizabethan* in November 1914 reported a good 12 months past and looked forward to fairly good football prospects ahead. The Great War, three months old, featured in the closing paragraphs. The effect of the war on the Officer Training Corps (OTC) had been to increase the number of recruits considerably. Two months later, the school magazine was printing the names of nearly 300 Old Elizabethans who were on active service with, already, four killed and six taken prisoner. By May of 1915, there was a

16-page supplement to the magazine with the casualty toll at nearly 30.

Numbers of boys on the College roll increased because it became less easy for parents to send their sons to England. As the months went by, the horrors of the Great War unfolded. At the Commemoration Service in 1916, the Principal read out a list of 44 Old Elizabethans already killed in action. Every edition of *The Elizabethan* added to the list – for some families it was not just one son lost, but two. Two O'Sheas, two Durands, two Marshalls, two Hills, two Myles, and the brothers Cox, killed in action within a month of each other in 1917.

No fewer than 662 Old Elizabethans served, 105 of whom were known to have been killed, many more dying subsequently of injuries sustained on the battlefield. Penney's stepson, Ralph Hawtrey (2555), was among them. Bill Rolleston, a master in the 1920s, came up with a chilling calculation: one in five of *all* the boys who had joined the College since the re-chartering in 1824 had served in the Great War.

School life between 1914 and 1918 carried on in much the same way as it always had, and although parts of the College field were dug up to grow potatoes and other vegetables, the usual matches and inter-collegiate clashes with Jersey went ahead. All improvements or repairs to buildings were put on hold, however, and what looked pretty shabby at the beginning of the war looked far worse at the end of it.

A page from the College's Book of Remembrance (above) and names on the World War I war memorial.

Perhaps the extent of the carnage and ghastliness of the trenches of Picardy had not yet hit home, but the number of trivialities the College authorities were dealing with, while the war progressed, seems extraordinary. The Royal Warrant Holders Association, for example, sent weekly letters in 1916 challenging the right of the College to use the Royal Coat of Arms over its main door. Other meetings of the Directors dealt with an elm tree, blown down on College land, which timber merchants were reluctant to buy, the problem solved only weeks later when the Principal himself finally offered to pay £3 for it. There were long discussions, too, in Directors' meetings about 'moral physiology' or sex education, the conclusions being that no instruction at all be given to boys under the age of 12 and no sexual information to boys under the age of 15.

Bigger issues came to the fore when the war was coming to an end. In 1918, the States agreed with Sir Michael Sadler that the College should become 'the crown of secondary education for boys in the island'. By then, though, Penney had been Principal for 30 years and there were signs that he was running out of steam. The energetic 27 year old who had taken the College by storm in the previous century was not, at 57, fired up in the same way. Whereas at one time he was equally at home in the classroom, the pulpit, the concert hall or on the playing field, he was now beginning to withdraw from involvement in any activity that was not wholly necessary.

The Directors knew they would soon have to appoint a new Principal, but there were equally pressing issues to consider. The expansion of the States Intermediate School for Boys, quickly establishing itself as a rival island school, was causing concern. At a special meeting in January 1921, the Directors noted that the Intermediate 'was growing in numbers, popularity and scope', with its promised new buildings 'the best of their kind in the island with accommodation for 300 to 400 boys'. None of this was helped by an Inspectors' report suggesting the College buildings were not fit for purpose.

Several questions were raised. Was it desirable to have two schools doing much the same work in competition with each other? Would it be possible to restrict the Intermediate, not originally intended to give secondary education, and, if so, would that be in the best interests of the island?

John Penfold, the Dean of Guernsey and Chairman of the Board, was an ardent educational reformer. He advocated a completely fresh start with the College housed in new buildings somewhere near the cricket field. Elizabeth College would be 'the centre for all secondary education for boys in the island and have the advantages of the Public School traditions of the College as well as those of a much larger and better school.'

Penfold was echoing an unpublished 1920 report by the Board of Education in England which had inspected the College for the first time. HM Inspectors condemned the badly planned and unsuitable buildings, noting that, among other deficiencies, there were 61 stairs from the bottom to the top of the main College. The boarding house, they said, was a serious fire risk: 'Instead of spending money on the present site, the right policy would seem to be the removal of the whole school and the erection of new and better buildings adjoining the playing fields as soon as conditions permit. It is recommended that the Principal's house and accommodation for boarders should be separate from the school.'

Spirits were lifted with a royal visit to the College by King George V and Queen Mary. They brought with them their only daughter, Princess Mary, who later became the Princess

The visit of King George V and Queen Mary in July 1921.

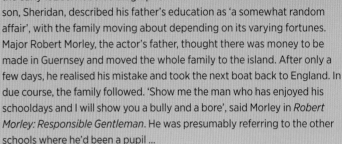

Robert Morley

Robert Morley (3579), the actor and comedian, was at the College briefly in the early 1920s. Robert's biographer son, Sheridan, described his father's education as 'a somewhat random affair', with the family moving about depending on its varying fortunes. Major Robert Morley, the actor's father, thought there was money to be made in Guernsey and moved the whole family to the island. After only a few days, he realised his mistake and took the next boat back to England. In due course, the family followed. 'Show me the man who has enjoyed his schooldays and I will show you a bully and a bore', said Morley in *Robert Morley: Responsible Gentleman*. He was presumably referring to the other schools where he'd been a pupil ...

Royal. The King inspected a guard of honour formed by the OTC, commanded by 'Chips' Littlewood, and two former service masters, Captain WCF Caldwell and FW Thelwall, who were presented to His Majesty. The long-serving former porter, Francis Hockaday, was also presented to the King and Queen. The highlight of the royal visit was the conferring of a knighthood on the Bailiff, Sir Edward Chepmell Ozanne (1445) in St George's Hall, the only time such a ceremony had been held in the island.

The time was fast approaching for William Penney to go. He had achieved a huge amount, not just for the College where six generations of boys had passed through his hands, but for education in the island generally. The College, which in 1889 had been regarded by certain sections as an 'octopus' and 'white elephant', had become, in Penney's own words, 'a crown and keystone in the island system'. His persuasive efforts led to the States adopting English scales of salaries and pensions for teachers island-wide.

Penney left Guernsey to become vicar of Norton Bavant, a tiny village in the rural heart of Wiltshire, where he remained for 20 years. It was just a stone's throw from the village of Stockton where Arthur Corfe had become rector when he was removed as Principal in 1868.

Norton Bavant church, and a Christmas card from the Revd Penney, 1923, marking his final Christmas at Elizabeth College.

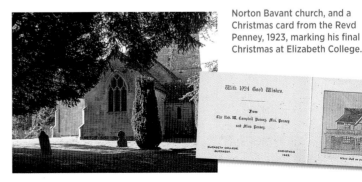

10

FELIX
UNHAPPY

'The Principal is inclined to be combative rather than conciliatory. He is an Irishman ... a born fighter ... with an aggressive attitude.'

HM INSPECTORS' REPORT ON FRANCIS HARDY, 1932

*I*N HIS INTERVIEW for the job as Principal in 1924, Francis Hardy, a house master at King Edward's, Bath, set out his stall. 'A school has no standing without discipline, corporal punishment is a necessary evil up to 15 years old, after which, if a boy cannot behave himself, he is better sent away.' Hardy declared himself keen on the OTC and games (which should not be compulsory) and he had a special interest in swimming and boxing. Mathematics, Classics and Latin were essentials and 'headmasters should take some part in every branch of the school'.

What he actually thought of the school as it stood, Hardy did not reveal during the interview, but he later described it as 'a ship without a rudder, drifting on a troubled sea'. He was highly critical of his predecessor, almost to the extent of

Cricket First XI, 1920. (Standing, from left to right) CW Foster (3409), CF Nason (3310), WK Mauger (3378), NL Wetherall (3255). (Seated) SA White (3289), VE Blad (3338), AD Ogilvy (3384), MDW Stonehouse (3347), JM Cohu (3408). (Front pair) GW Stone (3450), EA Savage (3466).

ungentlemanly conduct: 'The truth of the matter was that Mr Penney had been headmaster far too long … his energies had dissipated, his enthusiasm withered away and his outlook had become foggy and blurred.'

Hardy was scathing about the state of the buildings and classroom furniture. 'I began to plead with the Board for better facilities and working conditions. After a long struggle, rickety old desks were replaced by single-locker desks. Stout chairs took the place of splinter-bearing seats.' He regarded as a priority the installation of lighting and heating in classrooms where reading and writing were almost impossible after 3pm in the winter.

Above: The mailboat, *Alberta*, arrives at St Peter Port from Southampton. For mainland boarders, the six-hour crossing by steamer was the only means of travel. (Watercolour by Gilbert Holiday, c. 1922.)

Above right: Portrait of Dr Francis Hardy from the Le Marchant Room Collection.

The Guernsey social circuit was in full 1920s swing but Hardy turned his back on it: 'I had no time for cocktail parties or other such attractions and declined invitations which were showered upon me. I wanted to get on with the job.' The demands from Hardy for refurbishment, repair and modernisation came thick and fast as part of a large shopping list within 12 months of his taking over as Principal: a stage and a piano for the Hall; gas heating for the Ozanne Laboratory; bedrooms, dormitories and corridors to be redecorated; new entrance scholarships to be established and special scholarships for boarders; new lavatories and examination desks; and the acquisition of extra land for the College Field. He had one further request to make to the Directors at the end of his first 12 months – permission to go to Dublin University to receive a law doctorate, LLD.

Dr Hardy set about refurbishing outdated classrooms.

96

Hockey

Hockey became a recognised school sport in 1910 and the College was soon able to claim to have produced one of the greatest English hockey players, AD Ogilvy (3384). Ogilvy was capped for England from 1926 to 1935. An edition of the *Illustrated Sporting News* in 1936 described him as a supreme artist who 'at outside-left is as fine a sight as the hockey field has to offer'.

Matches started against Victoria College in 1924 after Dr Hardy, a keen hockey player himself, took personal charge of the game. Enthusiasm for the sport was rekindled after the exile years when RCN Roussel (4475), a graduate of Loughborough and Leicester county hockey player, returned

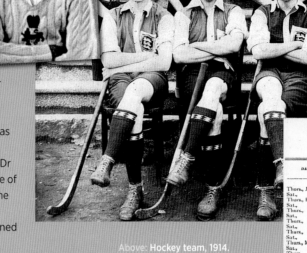

Above: **Hockey team, 1914.**

Inset: **AD Ogilvy.**

Left: **Adam Clark.**

ELIZABETH COLLEGE.
HOCKEY FIXTURES, 1915.

DATE.	OPPONENTS.	GROUND.	GOALS FOR	GOALS AG'ST	RESULT
Thurs., Jan. 28	Mr. Pontin's XI.	College			
Sat., „ 30	Guernsey Hockey Club	„			
Thurs., Feb. 4	Mr. Bachmann's XI.	„			
Sat., „ 6	Officers 2nd R.G.L.I.	„			
Thurs., „ 11	Athletics.	„			
Sat., „ 13	Mr. Waite's XI.	„			
Thurs., „ 18	Officers, Stafford Regt.	„			
Sat., „ 20	Mr. P. Peek's XI.	„			
Thurs., „ 25	Mr. Bachmann's XI.	„			
Sat., „ 27	Mr. Pontin's XI.	„			
Thurs., Mar. 4	Officers, 2nd R.G.L.I.	„			
Sat., „ 6	Athletics.	Morley College			
Thurs., „ 11	Guernsey Hockey Club	„			
Sat., „ 13	O.E.'s.				

Played............ Won............ Lost............ Drawn............

C. E. BLAD, Captain.
C. FRANK, Secretary.

to the College as a games and geography master. With his mentor, VG Collenette (4186), still on the staff, he took hockey in particular and sport in general to new heights at the College, and the replacement Pavilion at the Footes Lane Memorial Field, paid for by donors to the Elizabeth College Foundation, was named after him at its opening in 2010.

RD Self (4959) was Hockey Manager for the GB team which won a gold medal at the 1988 Olympics in Seoul, and he opened the new all-weather pitch at Foote's Lane in 1990.

In that decade, several Elizabethans were chosen for national teams, including BL Lanoe (8619), who was selected for the England Under 18 team. In 2008, AD Clark (9801) played in the England Under 16 team and a year later was promoted to the Under 18 squad.

By and large, Hardy's early wishes prevailed and at their meeting in November 1925, the Directors also decided on an early entry to the world of the phonograph record: 'A gramophone was placed in the Directors' room and two records were tried. It was agreed that the sum of eleven guineas be granted to cover the cost of purchase of a gramophone and records.' A new College cap was authorised with 'a Tudor Rose badge and St Andrew's Cross, a blue cap with white markings, the cap to be copyright and its use to be compulsory.'

A year later, the College was subject to its second assessment by HM Inspectors from the Board of Education in London. In the Principal, they liked what they saw. 'He is vigorous and a good organiser and he has established important reforms in the curriculum. Under his administration, there is every reason to anticipate a successful development of the School.'

The Inspectors gave an upbeat conclusion to their report: 'The general position of the school is very encouraging.' There was no further suggestion that the College should relocate to new buildings adjacent to the playing fields and the inspectors took note of big improvements in the present buildings, with plans for further renovation.

The inspectors would have seen for themselves that a new pavilion at the College Field had been built as a memorial to OEs lost in the Great War. A folding partition in the Hall, a memorial to Thomas Bushnell (1435), had been erected, and stained glass windows added to the rear of the stage area. The new gymnasium was opened by the Bailiff, Sir Havilland de Sausmarez (1775), in March 1927. Colonel GMH Colman (1834) had given a sizeable sum of money towards the project and the States paid the remainder.

Francis Hardy had little time for officialdom and was clearly a difficult man. In 1932, the Directors received a letter from the States Education Council complaining it was impossible to obtain information it needed from the Principal. Hardy was told that 'the business of the States should be attended to as expeditiously as possible and could ordinarily be settled by telephone'.

That same year, HM Inspectors, on their third visit to the College, noted 'an impalpable atmosphere of suppressed antagonism between the Headmaster and the Directors'. In remarks which were not included in the official report but are held in the National Archives at Kew, the Inspectors enlarged on their impressions of the Principal. 'He is inclined to stand on the letter of his rights under the Statutes and to be combative rather than conciliatory. He is an Irishman … a born fighter … with an aggressive attitude. He is jealous of the Intermediate School which he thinks engages the first affection of the States representatives.' It wasn't all bad, however, as the Inspectors also noted that the Directors 'appreciate his sterling merits and driving force within his own particular domain'.

The general view of Hardy's superiors seems to have been shared by many of his pupils. Two of them had distinguished careers in the services and were both, coincidentally, the sons of senior College masters and shared the Tupper Army Scholarship in 1939.

Major-General Francis (Griff) Caldwell (3873) described Hardy as 'a remarkable man who was tough, just what a headmaster should be. I liked him but he wasn't really a likeable man'.

Air Chief Marshal Sir Peter Le Cheminant (3946) saw Hardy as a man with

an enormous personality who struck fear into all of us including some masters. Popular he was not, but an effective Principal. He only caned me once – for breaking a rule that I didn't know even existed – that of travelling in a car driven

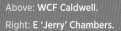

Left: Francis Hardy was a familiar figure on horseback, but earned the nickname 'Felix' when he stood, scowling, swinging his riding crop behind him in the manner of a cat's tail. Felix the Cat was popular in cartoons of the time.

Above: WCF Caldwell.
Right: E 'Jerry' Chambers.

by another boy. My caning was due on a Tuesday and proved abortive as it was an OTC day – 'I can't cane a boy in the King's uniform, come back tomorrow' – which I duly did.

Hardy's best performance – a serial one – was at the College Service in the Town Church which we attended in our Eton collars and waited for the reading – always the same one – which included the words 'Hooting of the Owls' rendered by him without fail as 'ooting of the howls'. Had applause been permitted it would have been thunderous.

Seventy years on, Sir Peter had other indelible memories of the College in the 1930s.

The masters were a fantasy – no one could have invented them or would believe in them now. 'Foxy' Rolleston, slightly drunk, used on occasion to read the Bible in Russian – accurately or not, no one knew. 'Bruggy' Waite, the Vice-Principal, had a beard and a vast stomach. He loved food and all things French and used to 'bog off' on the first days of the hols as did 'Chips' Littlewood, leaving his large north-country wife behind. On the day of his retirement, he left on the boat saying in his northern accent, 'I'll not kum back to this bluddy island again' and he never did. 'Micky' Manchester was a small or medium-sized boy's dream. Totally unable to keep even a semblance of order, he used to rant and roar totally ineffectually while his class became Bedlam – I was in my 'white mice' phase and exercised Roderick and Rhona in full view. Later, when cramming to get into Cranwell, I found him a great help and, of course, he has been a great benefactor to the College. 'Jerry' Chambers was dangerous, his temper always on a knife-edge. He'd had a bad war with most of his jaw shot away. We learnt from him as much from terror as anything else.

Caldwell was my first form master and he stood out, as did my own father, as being quiet and dignified and not good material for caricature or ragging. My father kept order by throwing well-aimed books and by illegal caning (only the Principal could cane legally) with OTC signalling sticks of which he broke several.

Sir Peter also recalled advice he received on the day he left Elizabeth College: 'On my leaving school, the headmaster's wife felt it incumbent on her to offer some worldly-wise advice. "Don't be taken in by all those nude women in nightclubs: they're not nude really, they're all wearing body stockings." Buttressed by this faulty intelligence, presumably vouchsafed by her husband, I felt ready to face the full rigours of adult life.'

In the summer of 1936, a further royal visit was in the offing with the possibility of the Prince of Wales calling on the College. The Board of Directors made plans for the visit and drew up the list of invitees. Hardy was not consulted, felt his authority had been usurped and told the Board that instead of receiving His Royal Highness he would be taking himself off for a day's fishing in Sark. The Board capitulated and, together with Major Caldwell, Hardy took on all the arrangements for what was a successful event.

Not long after his Guernsey visit, the Prince of Wales became king on the death of George V. By the time Britain had steered itself through the damaging abdication crisis, war in Europe loomed. Although the Channel Islands did not feel themselves to be completely immune from all the consequences of that, nothing had prepared them for what was soon to unfold.

Visit of the Prince of Wales, soon to become King Edward VIII, 1935.

THE EXILE YEARS

*'Today, I have seen a strange sight —
Elizabeth College caps and Ladies' College
uniforms and, too, a smattering of coloured
triangles on dark caps which told me the
Intermediate School was round about.'*

Victor Lewis, distinguished Fleet Street journalist,
reporting from the streets of Oldham

Francis Hardy had reached retirement age, was tired in the job and decided to resign: 'I have loved my work here but it is exacting and takes up nearly all my time. I am therefore looking forward to taking up less-exacting interests. A younger headmaster will be able to bring a fresh outlook and renewed vigour.'

What nobody could have quite foreseen in February 1939 was the combination of events that was to face Hardy's successor, that 'younger headmaster', in the first nine months of his tenure. WHG (Henry) Milnes — generations of boys also knew William Henry Goodenough Milnes as 'Bill' — took up his appointment in September 1939, the month war broke out.

German troops march past the Town Church. Occupying forces landed in Guernsey just days after the College had been evacuated to England.

Left: The Revd Henry Milnes.

Below: Micky Manchester.

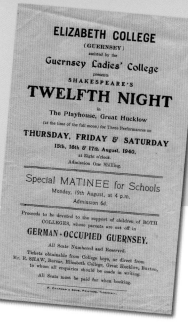

Right: Programme for *Twelfth Night*, organised to raise funds for people trapped on Guernsey.

Milnes had been on the staff of Uppingham School. Uncannily, Uppingham's Headmaster, John Wolfenden, had a sixth sense of what Milnes might have to face so soon into his new job. In the testimonial he provided with Milnes' application to become Principal, Wolfenden had written: 'He teaches Mathematics, Science and Divinity, but I know that he could equally well take several other branches of school work if necessary.' The testimonial continued almost as a prediction: 'Few events in school life, whether they were emergencies or matters of routine, could find him unprepared.'

At the age of 41, with a distinguished World War I record in the Royal Flying Corps, including the award of an MC, Milnes was on the brink of dealing with an emergency, the proportions of which nothing could have prepared him. There remains a dwindling band of Old Elizabethans who can still vividly remember the historic events of June 1940 when the College faced the biggest test of its long existence.

Winston Churchill's War Cabinet was considering whether the Channel Islands should be demilitarised and thus left wide open for occupation by German forces who had already entered Paris, only days after the rescue of 350,000 French and British troops from Dunkirk. In the House of Commons, Churchill warned of Hitler's plan to invade Britain: '… we shall defend our island whatever the cost may be. We shall fight on the beaches, we shall fight on the landing grounds, we shall fight in the fields and in the streets, we shall fight in the hills. We shall never surrender.'

What Churchill didn't say in that historic speech was that the government of mainland Britain would not defend or do anything about the Channel Islands. King George had a stark message to the Bailiffs of Guernsey and Jersey. 'For strategic reasons it has been found necessary to withdraw the armed forces from the Channel Islands. I deeply regret this necessity.' German invasion of British soil was imminent and the government at Westminster had little or no idea what to do. Its dealings with the Lt Governors and States officials were shambolic – the islands were effectively abandoned to the enemy.

Henry Milnes shone out of all this chaos as a beacon of practical sense. As VG Collenette (4186) recalled in his *Elizabeth College in Exile*: 'The speed of the German advance through France caught the Guernsey authorities unprepared; no plans were made for large-scale evacuation until the last minute. The Principal was probably more alive to the dangers inherent in the situation than anyone else.'

Milnes realised there was no time to lose. Somehow, not just the College but the entire school population of the island had to be moved out of Guernsey. France had fallen, the occupation of Guernsey by German forces was inevitable and getting closer by the hour.

The decision to evacuate was not simply a matter of moving a group of youngsters from one part of the country to another, as mainland schools had done, to avoid the blitz and bombing. For Guernsey families, Britain may have been the official mother country, but she was almost a foreign land.

There can be no better account of what happened in those momentous days in 1940 than from the pen of Milnes himself. The Milnes letter (see opposite page) written in August, two months after forced exile had begun, was probably intended for editors of English newspapers.

Accommodation in holiday chalets and the hangar of a gliding club in the Peak District village of Great Hucklow might have been acceptable in those summer holiday months of 1940. With a High Peaks winter just around the corner, there was a desperate need for something more permanent.

Elizabeth College
Great Hucklow
Tideswell
Derbyshire,
August, 1940.

Dear ... ,

When the enemy succeeded in crossing the Seine I felt that things looked rather serious for the Channel Islands so, as nobody seemed to be doing anything, I went to the Lt Governor to ask whether any scheme was in preparation for the evacuation of the schools.

Though some of those in authority doubted whether anything should be done, the Governor and the Procureur (Attorney General) saw my point and it was agreed that the Bailiff of Jersey, the Guernsey Procureur and I should fly to London to see the Home Office and that I should arrange the evacuation of the 30,000 children in the Channel Isles. Things had become so serious that the Governor of Jersey refused to allow the Bailiff to leave, and in the end, everything had to be arranged by telephone. My difficulty was that I was not allowed to say anything about the negotiations as the Government could not promise ships until they saw how the evacuation of the British Expeditionary Force went off. I, however, took a risk and got out a tentative scheme for the College.

At one stage, when we could hear the explosions from Cherbourg and other places on the French mainland and when our own military forces left the island, I almost gave up hope of the (rescue) boats. I booked passages for my wife and family on the Mailboat, resolving to stay myself with the College. Parents were getting very anxious and my telephone went night and day, so continuously, that I had to employ two helpers to take the calls.

As things turned out I was very glad that I had made thorough preparations as we had rather less than 24 hours' notice to move. We were brought over in a Dutch cargo boat, landed at Weymouth after an 11½ hours crossing and, put into a train bound for Oldham, of all places.

We arrived at 4 a.m. at Oldham, and at 9 a.m. I put through a call to the Ministry of Health in London from the Local Education Offices. The Oldham people had been expecting Belgian refugees and the arrangements were quite unsuitable for schools. I was, moreover, anxious to keep the College together as a unit and realised that although the people of Oldham were kindness itself, their climate was not the best thing for boys accustomed to breathing sea air. I organised the College on military lines, as we were living under camp conditions, making (Mickey) Manchester my adjutant and issuing daily orders. This made it more possible to leave the College while I made necessary arrangements. On Tuesday I got in touch with an M.P. who promised that if I got to the

-2-

House of Commons by 10 a.m. on Wednesday, he would make the Ministry see me.

The Ministry, when I actually got to them, were pleased to see me as they had no news of the College and other schools who had come with us. Everything was fixed up in about three quarters of an hour and orders sent to the Local Ministries at Manchester and Nottingham.

At present, the College and the Ladies' College, which I wished to keep with us as I thought it would be a good thing for brothers and sisters to be able to meet when they realised that they were cut off from their homes, are housed in Great Hucklow. The Ladies' College are in two very beautiful stone built holiday homes in the village. The College itself is partly in the holiday camp and partly in the quarters of a gliding club which lies above the village. The club is disused, as the authorities have ploughed up the landing ground.

It is a remote and lovely spot that we find ourselves in and for the summer the situation is, as the Ministry of Health said, about as healthy and safe a place as can be found in England. Great Hucklow is 1,000 feet above sea level and the gliding club 1,300 feet. The latter lies in the middle of a heather moor with marvellous views of distant hills in all directions. We are, of course, in the heart of the Peak District. The larger boys, who need more exercise, are in the gliding club premises and there are so many possibilities for enterprise, and they are so very full of energy, that I am sleeping up here with my wife in a caravan, to keep an eye on them. They have, I am glad to say, quite recovered from Oldham. We have improvised facilities for teaching, and HMI who visited us was most pleased with all our arrangements. Mr L du Garde Peach has placed his theatre in the village at our disposal and is to help in the production of a play. We have almost completed the construction of a swimming pool. Most of the College will have to play baseball instead of cricket as there are few level fields. The game is being taken up with much enthusiasm. A surprisingly large number of pets of varying origin have been collected in the space of a week, including two hedgehogs. Appetites are very good.

WHG MILNES. (Headmaster)

PS We shall be grateful for gifts of warm clothing, particularly boots or shoes; for loans of beds, bedding, chairs and tables; and for contributions towards the camp fund for the benefit of boys who are cut off from their parents.

Any assistance towards keeping the games going, cricket, hockey, football, and indoor games will be most welcome.

Top: The hangar at the gliding club at Great Hucklow.

Left: The *Batavier IV* took many evacuees from Guernsey to Weymouth.

Above left: White Hall main entrance.

Above: Unpacking on arrival.

Left: Elizabeth Grantham, née Milnes.

Milnes resisted attempts to join the College with other schools and turned down offers to have boys taken in by local families. Eventually, he succeeded in securing the lease on a large country house, White Hall, three miles outside Buxton. While the Senior School established itself at White Hall, the Juniors were found more substantial buildings in the village of Great Hucklow, the stone-built Florence Nightingale Homes.

The wonder is that Milnes and his staff were able to keep the College together at all, let alone begin a near-normal school term on 1 October 1940. In a report to the emergency Board of Directors, Milnes was later to enlarge on the College experience in Oldham, a hitherto unpublished account of the severe problems the College community was having to endure.

'The conditions in which we found ourselves at Oldham were unbelievably bad … the sleeping conditions were definitely dangerous. There were no beds, merely mattresses on the floor … there was no ventilation. There was dust and grime everywhere and the situation suggested alarming possibilities such as infection of some serious nature, cerebro-spinal meningitis, for example.'

Elizabeth (Milnes) Grantham, the Principal's daughter, was later to remember arriving at Great Hucklow. 'After Oldham, which was black, I couldn't help but roll in the grass at Hucklow. Seventy years later, I can still remember the smell of that lovely, lovely grass.'

Milnes, meanwhile, was coping with problems from an enemy within, namely, some of the masters' wives who 'were making ill-informed criticism about the efforts being made at Great Hucklow'. Writing to Louis Cohen (2652), Chairman of the wartime Directors, in November 1940, Milnes explained the disturbing effect exile from Guernsey was having on some of the teaching staff.

'An upheaval such as the evacuation does exaggerate weakness of character and my experience of somewhat similar conditions in the last world war prepared me for some of the failures which occurred.' Three members of staff, he said, who'd been afflicted by events had begun to 'recover their morale', but this wasn't the case with their wives.

> Mrs Littlewood has to my knowledge been guilty of breaches of etiquette. She wrote, without reference to me, a letter to the press at Oldham purporting to represent the views of the College. Much in this letter I would not have sanctioned had I been consulted. She has been responsible for statements which, unless I had intervened, might have led to legal action … one or two other wives have shown themselves to be nearly equal makers of mischief.

It's not clear what statements might have led to legal action but, to be fair to the wives concerned, Milnes was nothing if not an autocrat: he was fearful of losing control if the wives had too much contact with the evacuee parents who'd moved to Derbyshire to be near their sons.

Difficult though times were, OEs themselves have talked of a sense of adventure and excitement. Victor Collas (4014), who had his 17th birthday just before that first term

began at White Hall, said separation was far worse for the parents: 'When I said goodbye to my mother, she burst into tears. I've never forgotten that.'

Astonishingly, in all the accounts of those exile years, emotional moments such as that are rarely recorded. Nobody was aware of it at the time, but when the school children said goodbye on the quayside in Guernsey, it was the beginning of five years of near-complete isolation from their parents. For that reason, perhaps, accounts of preparations for evacuation and the first weeks and months in Derbyshire reveal few inner feelings and emotions on the part of those involved. Today, the separation of children from their families, in the manner that Guernsey children were taken away from their homes in 1940, would raise an international outcry. And yet, as recently discovered correspondence reveals, some parents were clearly more worried about their possessions than about members of their family as they prepared for evacuation.

CMY Trotter (4180) described the College preparations for evacuation.

> I spent the evening packing as much as I could into a large suitcase, while mother hid the silver in odd corners round the house. Father gave me the most valuable part of his stamp collection, together with my birth certificate and savings certificates, addresses of friends and relations in England, and £12 (all he had in the house at the time).
>
> We had to carry our suitcases down to the harbour as there was no transport available. During this, the handle of my suitcase came off – you can imagine how I felt trying to carry a very heavy suitcase, containing about £500 worth of stamps, with no handle.

Trotter says senior boys found something to celebrate on the train which had met them at Weymouth: 'We went by special train to Oldham. To commemorate our journey, when we reached the Severn Tunnel, the prefects opened a bottle of champagne and a bottle of port which had been rescued from the officers' mess at Fort George [Guernsey's former army garrison].'

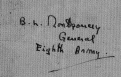

Field Marshal Montgomery was a relative of NDW Thomas (4211) and wrote personally to him at Buxton in 1943. Monty's address was simply 'Eighth Army'.

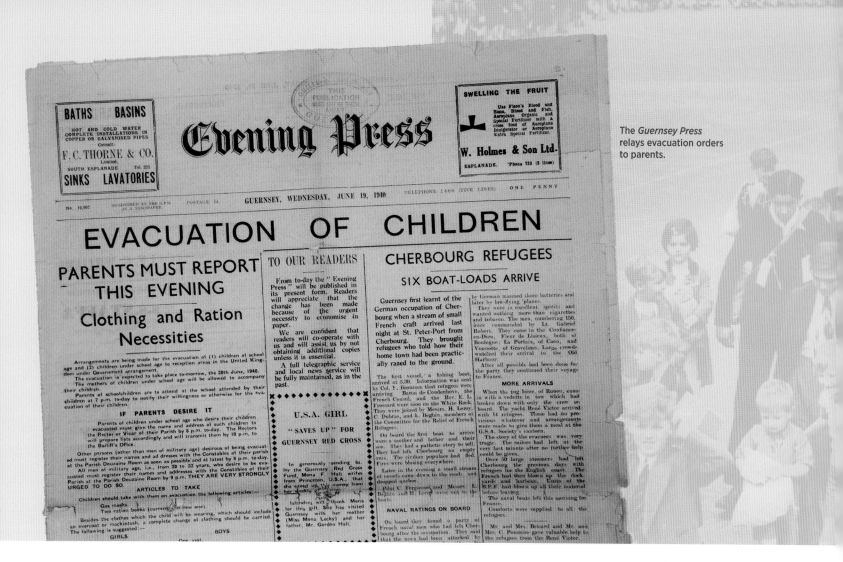

Back in Guernsey, Trotter's parents, James and Margaret, were among those who had decided to follow their children and leave the island as the threat of German occupation became more of a reality and changed from 'if' to 'when'. But in her diary account of the days leading up to their departure, Margaret Trotter is not only concerned about Charles.

> June 19th. Elizabeth College decided on evacuation. States decided on evacuation for other island schools ... I picked up the best of our silver and put it in an inconspicuous place. My son brought home a list of things he must take, all going into one suitcase, and I got this ready.
>
> June 20th. Got my son off, with suitcase, and enough food for three meals. The Germans might be here at any minute. Some panic in town – banks only allowing withdrawals of £20 and long queues. The town is full of posters, 'Don't Be Yellow', 'Business As Usual', 'The Rumour that Compulsory Evacuation has been ordered is a LIE!'
>
> Met the Procureur's wife (May Sherwill) and said, 'Are you going tonight as planned and have your children gone?' She said, 'No, I have decided to stay with my husband and I couldn't let the two youngest go off with the schools so I'm keeping them with me.'

On 28 June, the Trotters sailed on the last ferry out of Guernsey which had been strafed by the Luftwaffe at its berth in St Peter Port harbour. Margaret's diary records:

> It was a very crowded boat but we luckily got across safely and arrived in London in the afternoon of 29 June. The news that the Germans occupied Guernsey on the 30th was a sad blow although it was then expected. We can get no news of those left behind.

In Guernsey, the Procureur himself, Ambrose Sherwill, had attempted to get a letter to a senior Home Office official asking for help from London to deal with the unfolding events. The letter ended: 'Could you, as a personal favour, drop a line to my boy of 15, Richard F Sherwill, Elizabeth College, c/o Education Office, Oldham and say that his mother and I and Joly and Rollo are quite well and send their love ...' The letter was never delivered.

Several weeks later, meanwhile, Charles Trotter's father, James, was still concerned about his stamp collection and eventually wrote to his son, by now in the improvised accommodation in Derbyshire.

> We have brought over the rest of your clothes in your cabin trunk. Ask Milnes if we should send them on or keep them.

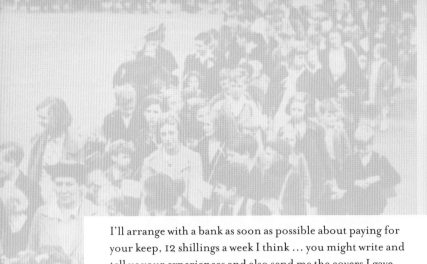

I'll arrange with a bank as soon as possible about paying for your keep, 12 shillings a week I think … you might write and tell us your experiences and also send me the covers I gave you to look after. I hope the stamp album is safe, keep it at present. I've brought over the other albums and have arranged that some of my books and Japanese swords are to be stored at Lovell's [Guernsey furniture depository].

Keep smiling,

Your affectionate father.

It might all have seemed callous but Elizabeth Grantham says there was an attitude within the school as a whole (which included the families of masters) of 'putting up with things for the duration'. Another factor, she says, was casualties — some boys who had only recently left school had been killed in action. Self-pity was not on the agenda.

Life in exile settled down to a workable routine. From the start, improvised classrooms doubled up as dining rooms; there was no playing field and no gym. It all tested the

Breakfast in Oldham Co-operative Hall, June 1940.

ingenuity of boys and staff and conditions improved term by term. A lack of domestic staff meant the boys washed up, cleaned and swept rooms, lit fires, maintained boilers and fed the chickens. There was probably no harm done by that.

Vernon Collenette's *Elizabeth College in Exile* remains the most authoritative account of the school's time in Derbyshire. His widow, Thelma, has had a lifetime connection with the College and, as the daughter of a master, was at Great Hucklow in the exile years.

We had no idea what was happening in Guernsey and we heard nothing about the treatment of other occupied

Left and opposite: White Hall in winter; and summer pursuits.

Red Cross messages.

countries … The horrors only came to us after the war. Yes, we missed our homes, friends and relations but it was those left behind who did the worrying. Where were their children? Who was looking after them? Had they enough clothes and money? When would they see them again? That must have been terrible for the parents. Once the Red Cross messages started, limited to no more than twenty words, some of the questions were answered. Even then one had to be careful. Vernon's contained news of a school nature – cricket, exams etc. and the replies mention growing vegetables, keeping rabbits and chicks for eggs and 'we are ok'.

Bizarrely, the Red Cross messages sent by the boys to their families in Guernsey had to be picked up at the main College building in St Peter Port which from early on in the occupation had become the Red Cross bureau. JA Davis (4279), who remained in the north of England for a career as a teacher and headmaster in Oldham, has added postscripts to already published accounts of life in Derbyshire.

He remembers Tuffy Thompson, the Maths master, teaching in a hangar of the Yorkshire and Derbyshire Gliding Club and using the sides of glider containers as blackboards. He described bath-time thus: 'We had a weekly bath in the Club House kitchen. Lining up form by form, the first one received a pail of hot water in a galvanised bath. Two minutes in and then out and more water added with the next boy in. If you were last, you had plenty of dirty water. Start again for the next form.'

For Guernsey boys, the arrival of heavy snow was a delightfully new experience, but with some drawbacks. 'In January 1941 we were told that as we had missed our full summer holiday, we could have two weeks free of lessons to

dawn. This was uneventful except on one occasion. The Principal received a telephone call asking us to search for an Anson training plane which had crashed in the fog. We eventually found it, but the army had got there first. We suggested that they might like to go to a nearby farmhouse for their breakfast, to which they readily agreed, whilst we looked after the plane. On arriving back in the 6th form, we discovered that we had all brought back souvenirs. There was the distress pack which, had the plane crashed in the sea, turned a large circle of water bright orange to make it more easily visible for would be rescuers. It was put in the river which flowed through Buxton causing much interest.

enjoy the snow. The only rub was that we had to spend the whole day outside apart from mealtimes.'

Davis also tells the story of a hardly-to-be-forgotten schoolboy escapade:

> As members of the OTC at the age of 16 we became members of the Home Guard. Apart from normal parades and drill, we had to undertake early morning patrols from

Above and below: Home Guard Patrols.

There was a large amount of machine gun ammunition. This was disintegrated and the powder used to fill empty Quink ink bottles. At the top of each bottle an empty cotton reel with a nail through a hole in the centre was fastened and weighted. Some card wings were stuck on and when it was lobbed through the air onto the hard tennis court a reasonable explosion followed.

Someone had also brought the Verey pistol and flares which, when fired, lit up the night sky. I think we thought we'd got away with it but another group, from Buxton College, had taken the log book and maps and it was these the authorities were interested in.

Monsieur Waite (Vice-Principal and French Master) had always warned us when we failed to agree tenses, genders or similar *grosses fautes*, that we would end up in the arms of the law. So when, some weeks later, the local bobby arrived on his bicycle outside the Lower VI form room where we were having French, Monsieur Waite's day was made. He had the biggest of smiles to know that his prophecy had come to pass and we were summoned to appear in court.

Thanks to the Principal, we were spared as he went to court on our behalf. He was fined two or three pounds and we were fined 2/6d [12.5p] each which meant no pocket money for five weeks.

After a lifetime in the teaching profession, John Davis takes a kindly, retrospective and undoubtedly deserved view of the masters at White Hall and Great Hucklow.

My best memory is of the unfailing kindness of the staff (at a time when their own personal lives must have been under great stress) as well as the responsibility of teaching and caring for such a large number of boys in very difficult circumstances for twenty four hours a day, e.g. 'Mrs Chips' [Littlewood's wife] meeting us as we came from Buxton College where we went for Science lessons. She would say to a boy, 'That pullover looks grubby, take it off and put this one on. I'll wash it and give it back to you next week'. Or 'Chips' taking a fifth form Science lesson at White Hall, 'Sherwill, you are a fool, an absolute fool'. Dick (Sherwill) had, I think, used the wrong chemical formula.

The bell goes for end of lesson.

Chips: 'Happy birthday, Dick! Mrs "Chips" sent you this', giving him a small present.

Newspaper reports by Victor Lewis.

The Daily Sketch

KEMSLEY HOUSE, LONDON, W.C.1.
TELEPHONE: TERMINUS 1234
WITHY GROVE, MANCHESTER 4
TELEPHONE: BLACKFRIARS 1234

THIS IS URGENT 1943

THE *Daily Sketch* has disclosed that 70,000 people in the German-occupied Channel Islands are threatened with starvation. These are British subjects, thousands of whose sons and daughters are serving voluntarily in our forces.

It is sincerely to be hoped that while we liberate foreign lands, we shall be able to do something for these sorely tried people waiting despairingly in the only spot in the British Empire occupied by the Nazi.

The German garrisons in the islands are completely isolated. There is no way of escape, and they are small in numbers. Sooner or later those Germans must become prisoners. We shall then have to feed them.

We commend to the consideration of the authorities a suggestion that we send certain limited supplies to the Germans on condition that they will allow us to send food ships to the islanders on the same principle as was adopted in Greece.

The relative cost of saving 70,000 Britons from starvation under this plan would be so small that it should

BRITISH DRUGS FOR CHANNEL ISLANDERS

By Daily Sketch Correspondent, VICTOR LEWIS

A LARGE consignment of drugs and medical necessities, including 400,000 units of insulin, has reached Nazi-occupied Jersey and Guernsey from Britain, it was learned last night.

But the food situation is still causing anxiety, proof of which is added by deportees.

Advocate A. J. Sherwill, Attorney-General of Guernsey when the island was seized, who is now in a German prison camp, says in a letter:

"According to a German notice, British activities are having the effect of preventing supplies of essentials and rations are being cut.

"My wife (who is still in the island)...

School For Heroes

From VICTOR LEWIS, 'Daily Sketch' Air Correspondent

WON EVERY AWARD UP TO THE V.C.

EVERY military award, from the Victoria Cross to a Mention in Dispatches, has been won in this war by boys of Elizabeth College, Guernsey's exiled public school, which to-day carries on in a little Derbyshire village.

When, yesterday, it was announced that a George Medal had been awarded to "Nicky" Carey, son of an island bank manager, for displaying "resource, courage, determination and cool judgment in the highest degree," the all-in list of medals was completed.

With the Army, Navy, R.A.F., Fleet Air Arm, Merchant Navy and Civil Defence, Old Elizabethans have won 16 decorations.

In the years before the war, six boys sat side by side in the sixth form of that island school. Every one of them has been decorated—seven medals between them.

One was Major Wallace Le Patourel, son of Guernsey's Attorney-General at that time. After being "posthumously" awarded the V.C. it was learnt that he was alive—wounded and a prisoner. Later he was repatriated.

His classmates included:

Capt. F. G. Caldwell, son of the present head of the Lower School, who won the M.C. and Bar;

Major A. L. Laxton, son of an island minister, M.C.;

Brian Westland Rose, of the Fleet Air Arm, one of the few survivors of the famous Swordfish attack on the Scharnhorst and Gneisenau in the Channel. Rose, who has since been killed, won the D.S.O.;

Lieut. L. L. Stone, son of a Guernsey tobacconist, M.M.;

M. F. Harding, Fleet Air Arm, D.S.C.

Two old boys have won the D.F.C., two have won the D.F.M., and three have been "mentioned."

The College was lucky to have had many friends on the mainland to promote its needs and interests both at the crucial time when accommodation had to be found, quickly, and then throughout its time in Derbyshire when the College needed to try to maintain an ordinary existence. Among them were the retired Principal, Dr Hardy, and two distinguished OEs, VA Grantham (2866) and E Gibson Fleming (2894).

Victor Lewis was a part-time cricket coach at the College in the 1930s. Also a reporter on the *Guernsey Star,* he became its editor before heading for Fleet Street in 1937. By chance, he was Northern News Editor of the national newspaper *The Daily Sketch* at the very moment he could use his journalistic influence. He had an extraordinary opportunity to keep the fate of islanders, and the College in particular, in the public eye. In 1940, before the Germans

had suppressed news from Britain in Guernsey, he was able to write for Guernsey's local papers:

> Today, I have walked through the streets of Oldham and seen a strange sight — Elizabeth College caps and Ladies' College uniforms and, too, a smattering of coloured triangles on dark caps which told me the Intermediate School was round about.
>
> Down in the Co-Operative Hall in King Street, I have heard the cheering voices of Captain Eric Chambers and Mr FG Manchester, Elizabeth College masters, setting about the task of converting this strange building into some internal resemblance of the castellated edifice which looks down on the town of St Peter Port.
>
> I am at the disposal of any Guernsey parent who feels that I can do anything at all to ease their anxiety. If you want to know how Willie is, just write to me, tell me where he is, and I'll do the rest.

Throughout the war, Victor Lewis kept the plight of evacuees on the pages of the national press in Britain.

He never forgot Elizabeth College — he'd married a Guernsey girl, Maisie Mackay, and his two brothers-in-law were AM Mackay (3354) and AFS Mackay (3801). Victor's son Lynn Lewis (4467) joined the College in Derbyshire.

In January 1945, by then an Air Correspondent, Lewis was able to write in the *Daily Sketch*: 'Every military award, from the Victoria Cross to a Mention in Despatches, has been won in this war by Elizabeth College, Guernsey's exiled public school, which today carries on in a little Derbyshire village.'

After five long years, liberation came for the Channel Islands. The nation tuned into wireless sets to listen to Churchill. His words still ring in the ears of many Guernsey evacuees: 'Hostilities will end officially at one minute after midnight tonight, but in the interests of saving

Left: Boys in chapel and a plan of White Hall by GP Warley (4335).

Right: The Buxton Chapel Cross was brought back to Guernsey.

lives the "Cease Fire" began yesterday to be sounded all along the front, and our dear Channel Islands are also to be freed today.'

Lynn Lewis, seven years old and the youngest in the school, remembers celebrating VE Day

> by throwing our pillows around the three-boy dormitory and rushing up and down the corridor – without even getting told off! The next morning, we were told we were being taken to join the real big boys in Buxton to celebrate. I don't think I even knew there was a senior school. For a seven year old it was enough to look up to the bigger boys aged 11 to 13 of forms II and III who impressed us so much without contemplating that there could be even bigger boys.

> I was put in the care of GE Heggs (4151), who filled me with awe – no less than when he became Head Prefect the next year when we were back in Guernsey. Looking back, I am not surprised he became a revered Judge of the British Industrial Tribunal process and a Recorder.

> Heggs – I am now actually allowed to address him as Geoffrey at OE dinners in London – took me out in a seven-feet-long paddle-boat on the biggish pond that they

Above: The King's Proclamation to the island, read on the College steps by Brigadier Snow, flanked by the Bailiff and States members.

Below: Milne's address to College, January 1945.

JANUARY. 1945.

WE ARE AT THE BEGINING OF A NEW YEAR. A YEAR IN WHICH WE MAY REASONABLY HOPE TO SEE AN END TO OUR EXILE AND A REALIZATION OF THE HOPE SO OFTEN DEFERRED.

IN THESE YEARS THE COLLEGE HAS GREATLY DISTINGUISHED ITSELF. OLD ELIZABETHANS, SCHOLARS, AND STAFF HAVE ALL PLAYED A VALIANT PART, AND AS A RESULT THE COLLEGE IS MORE WIDELY KNOWN AND ITS PRESTIGE HIGHER THAN PERHAPS EVER BEFORE IN ITS HISTORY. I WOULD ASK ALL TO SEE THAT WE FINISH THIS EPISODE WITH THE SAME RESOLVE AND WITH THE SAME SPIRIT WITH WHICH WE BEGAN.

OUR RETURN, WHEN IT COMES, MAY TEST THE COLLEGE AS THOROUGHLY AS THE ORIGINAL EVACUATION. I KNOW THAT ALL OF YOU WILL WISH TO DO YOUR PART. THERE ARE THREE THINGS THAT YOU ALL CAN ATTEND TO.

FIRST SEE THAT THERE IS NO SLACKNESS IN YOUR OWN DISCIPLINE, SO THAT YOU DO NOT BRING DISCREDIT TO THE COLLEGE AT ANY TIME BY NEGLECTING YOUR APPEARANCE OR YOUR MANNERS.

SECONDLY BE CHEERFUL. AVOID GROUSING AND BEING CYNICALLY CLEVER. THIS NEVER REALLY HELPS AND IS A NUISANCE WHEN THINGS HAVE TO BE DONE.

THIRDLY KEEP YOUR EYES OPEN, AND WHEN YOU SEE SOME- -THING TO BE DONE DO IT. DO NOT PASS IT ON TO SOMEONE ELSE, EVEN IF IT IS NOT YOUR TURN. IF WE ALL DO AS MUCH AS WE CAN I BELIEVE THERE IS A GREAT FUTURE FOR THE COLLEGE AND HAPPINESS FOR US ALL.

FLOREAT COLLEGIUM.

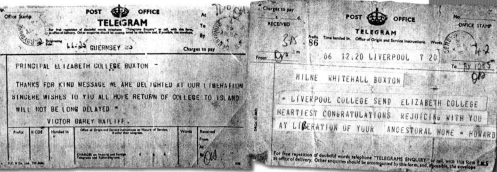

still glorify by terming it a 'lake' in the town. Heggs turned the paddles and it went so fast that I asked him if it was possible to go in it across the sea to Guernsey. He let me have a turn but the boat just spun in circles when I, quite reasonably, turned both the handles clockwise.

In Guernsey itself, the day after VE Day, the granite stairway leading to the main door of Elizabeth College was chosen for Brigadier Alfred Snow to read the Royal Proclamation vesting in him the powers of military commander. With the union flag hoisted high between the towers above the Le Marchant Library, the band of the Duke of Cornwall's Light Infantry, which had arrived in the island only that morning, marched through the College gates playing the Old Comrades march.

A huge, cheering audience of nearly 3,000 islanders then heard Brigadier Snow read a message from the King welcoming Guernsey back to its rightful place with the free nations of the world: 'Channel Islanders in their thousands are fighting in my service for the cause of civilisation … their task is not yet ended: but for you a new task begins at once — to rebuild the fortunes of your beautiful Islands in anticipation of reunions with relatives, friends, and neighbours who have been parted from you by the circumstances of war.'

Recent research by Gillian Mawson has highlighted difficult questions faced by boys returning from Derbyshire, such as, 'Were you one of those who stayed or ran away?' One recalls how his father, who had also been an evacuee, found it difficult to get a job.

> My father was told to his face by his supervisor that he would not be given the 'best' jobs because they were going to people who had remained and suffered during the Occupation, whereas he had chosen to run off to England. I will never forget how upset our whole family were at this treatment.

At the beginning of the Occupation, the College buildings had been taken over by the States Controlling Committee, but in 1941 they were requisitioned by the German authorities. Several offices were set up, one of which was for the issue of permits.

JC Sauvary, a builder and St Sampson's churchwarden, kept a diary of the Occupation. His entry for 16 March 1942, reads:

Today I had to go to Elizabeth College for a permit for coffin material. While I was waiting (to see an officer), I saw a picture of Hitler over the desk … I lost my way coming out and found myself in the basement. It's unbelievable down there. It's distressing to see Elizabeth College occupied, especially remembering Speech Days of the past.

July 1942:

The Germans are fixing rails from the White Rock to St Sampson. I went to Elizabeth College again yesterday for a permit for timber. It is heartbreaking to see the old College.

A strongroom bunker was built by the Germans inside the old boarders' room, now the AJ Perrot room. It remains there, but had its door removed in the 1990s for safety reasons.

The German officer responsible for building fortifications in the Channel Islands, Generalmajor Rudolf Schmetzer, was based in the College and his survey led directly to Hitler's order that the islands be turned into 'impregnable fortresses', the legacy of which is still clear for all to see around the coastlines of the Channel Islands.

In 1939, an air raid shelter had been built for the school under the tennis courts in front of the College.

THE DASH
The Newsletter Of The Channel Dash Association

Volume 1 Issue 2   www.channeldash.org   **Summer 2008.**

Channel Dash Spotlight

Brian Westland Rose DSO.

Brian was the pilot of Swordfish W5983 during the attempt to prevent the German battle fleet passing through the Dover Straits on 12 February 1942. His Observer was Sub Lt Edgar Lee and at the rear was TA/G Leading Airman A L Johnson. Brian's aircraft was second in line behind Esmonde's as they went in for the attack. During the approach the aircraft was hit by canon shell splinters which caused significant damage to the aircraft and had split the fuel tank covering the crew with petrol which, fortunately did not ignite. Brian was severely wounded in the back by the canon shell but managed to keep the aircraft flying and release their torpedo. Brian switched over to the reserve fuel tank which would give them a further ten to twelve minutes flying time, however, the aircraft was losing height and Brian struggled to keep it flying. The Aircraft flew over the stern of the Gneisenau as they turned to starboard in order to try and avoid the anti aircraft fire from the ships. As Brian concentrated on keeping the aircraft flying Edgar had turned and saw that TA/G 'Ginger' Johnson was slumped over his machine gun. He had been mortally wounded by the exploding canon shell which had hit the aircraft earlier in the attack. Meanwhile the aircraft was still losing height and Brian was able to make a controlled crash landing on the sea about half a mile from the Prinz Eugen. As the aircraft started sinking Edgar was able to help Brian escape into the dinghy before their Swordfish disappeared below the surface taking the body of 'Ginger' Johnson with it. Brian and Edgar (continued on page 4)

Lieutenant Brian Rose DSO RNVR

Brian Rose

One evening at Great Hucklow, 'Jerry' Chambers, a master not known for his even temper, surprised a group of boys just before lights out. Among the group was R Champion (4388). 'Jerry came in quietly: he had tears streaming down his cheeks and said he wanted to share something with us. "We've lost Brian Rose. Watling's gone and now it's Rose."'

Although killed later in an air accident, Rose had actually survived one of the most ferocious air battles of the war. As the strongest force ever put to sea by Hitler attempted to flee up the English Channel, past the Dover Straits into home waters, six obsolete Swordfish biplanes had been ordered by Admiral Sir Bertram Ramsay to take on the German armada – two battleships, a heavy cruiser, with escorts afloat and in the air. All six Swordfish were shot down, but not before heroic action by their crews. Brian Rose (4059) was one of the Swordfish pilots – the fuel tank of his aircraft was hit by shell splinters, Brian was shot in the back, but he kept the aircraft flying long enough to fire

The painting 'Channel Dash Heroes', by Philip E West, depicting the rescue of Brian Rose in the English Channel. It was commissioned by his fellow OE, Rob Champion.

its torpedo. After a controlled crash landing, he was dramatically rescued by motor torpedo boat and subsequently awarded the DSO.

Rob Champion was so moved by that evening at Great Hucklow and the sheer emotion displayed by Captain Chambers that he retained a lifelong interest in what is known today as 'The Channel Dash' – in his words it was 'burned on his soul'. He commissioned a painting of Brian Rose's rescue in the Channel.

It was not until 1 August 1945, when circumstances allowed, that the boys were able to return to the island. German prisoners of war had been detailed to clean up the College classrooms and corridors and make good the damage done to the fabric itself, which was not as bad as had been feared.

A 70th anniversary event was organised in 2010 when a number of exiles, by now in their mid-80s, returned to Great Hucklow and White Hall. For some, it was as if they had never been away. 'I was caught by Henry Milnes, there in Dorm 3, having a pillow-fight with Wilson Gaudion!' Geoffrey Heggs exclaimed as he walked into White Hall. D de P Robert (4454) confessed: 'Actually, they were the happiest moments of my life. I suddenly felt free, after Guernsey.' John Davis said that when they boarded the cattle boat in St Peter Port harbour, they didn't have a clue where they were going, except to Weymouth. 'We were told we might be going to Canada and when my parents heard that, they burst into tears.'

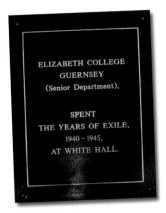

The plaque in White Hall commemorating the years of exile.

The collective memory of those OE exiles, returning to Derbyshire after so many years away, was that they did not suffer any real deprivation. John Davis freely admitted the experience had made a man of him. 'I was a bit of a mummy's boy and although my parents were loving, they were Victorian and disciplinarians. Coming here gave me independence and I grew up immediately.'

The years in exile may have been the most momentous event in the history of Elizabeth College, but Milnes knew, and the Directors were soon made aware, that there were even more pressing matters ahead.

Sir Ambrose Sherwill, KBE

The Procureur of Guernsey at the outset of the war was later to become one of the island's most distinguished Bailiffs, Sir Ambrose Sherwill (3079). Sherwill won the MC for bravery on the Western Front in 1917 and was wounded several times.

Resuming his career in law back in Guernsey after the end of World War I, he became HM Comptroller and then HM Procureur in 1935. When the island was occupied, he was the natural choice as President of the Controlling Committee. His impeccable World War I record gained him the respect of the senior German officers in charge of the island's occupying forces. However, after a series of episodes involving covert landings by British army officers in Guernsey (most of them OEs), Sherwill was stripped of his position as President of the Controlling Committee and sent to prison in France, first in Versailles and then in the Cherche Midi in Paris.

He became Bailiff of Guernsey in 1946 and subsequently received two knighthoods.

Seventy years on, former 'exiles', their families and other OEs gather in Buxton for a weekend of commemorative events.

12

HOME
AT LAST

'The Directors should realise that in 1939 the College was probably finished as a public school. This was not realised by the Directors or by anyone else in the island.'

THE PRINCIPAL, IN AN ADDRESS TO THE DIRECTORS, 1953

HE FIRST MEETING of the Directors after the liberation in 1945, before the College as a whole moved back to Guernsey, was extraordinarily matter of fact. The minutes of the meeting simply record that the Chairman 'stressed how throughout the past five years the College had upheld its reputation both academically and in sport'.

In truth, too much dwelling on the past in the immediate post-war years would have been a mistake. The island was picking itself up, the old order in Guernsey swept away by five years of occupation by enemy forces.

In spite of the College being kept together as a viable community in a never-to-be-forgotten way throughout the war years, there were near-insurmountable difficulties ahead, the most pressing of these to do with status and finance.

HM the Queen with Principal Milnes on her visit to the College in July, 1957.

Left: Filling the bunker after the German occupation.

Below: Tennis court construction 1954.

Inset: Prefect's cap badge.

Outlining fears to the Board in his usual forthright fashion, the Principal didn't mince words: 'The Directors should, I think, realise that in 1939 the College was, probably, finished as a public school. This was not realised by the Directors or by anyone else in the island.'

In Britain, the mark of a 'public school' is generally taken to be membership of the Headmasters' Conference or HMC. Technically, the headmaster himself is the member of the HMC and must reapply on behalf of the school when appointed to his post. Milnes revealed that when he went through the formalities in 1939, he was told Elizabeth College no longer qualified for membership and, to his horror, the HMC turned him down: the College had ceased to meet the requirements of independence largely because of its funding arrangements. Had it not been for the impending catastrophe for the Channel Islands in 1940, Milnes admitted he would have packed his bags and gone back to England.

In the event, during its exile in Derbyshire, the College was readmitted to the HMC, partly because of its special wartime difficulties but also the willingness of other HMC members to offer their support. Back on home territory, the College once again faced HMC rejection because of its financial arrangements with the States. Milnes impressed on the Directors how important it was to remain a member of the 'club'. The different status of HMC and non-HMC schools attracted a different set of masters, he claimed, and the impact of non-membership would be felt not only in the classroom, but also on the games field:

Prep schools which are now sending boys to us would stop doing so ... parents in Guernsey would choose public schools on the mainland ... the best qualified members of staff, if they cherished any ambitions, would begin to make frantic attempts to move to other schools.

Princess Elizabeth inspecting the CCF at the White Rock, 1949.

Beechwood 1960s.

Milnes told the Directors the problem would be solved only if the Bailiff and the States could be persuaded to award a block grant to the College with, most importantly, the College retaining control of how it was spent. He ended his long monologue to the Directors with these words:

> If the right decisions are taken now, the prospect before the College is more favourable than it has been for perhaps 50 years or even at any time. If the opportunity is missed, I should not be surprised to see an accelerating decline in the fortunes of the College so that in ten or 12 years' time, it would probably be hardly recognisable as the same institution.

It took several years to achieve the system of financing that Milnes was advocating. In 1958, the States passed a resolution 'that the financial assistance afforded to the College shall be in the form of an annual Block Grant' and that the Combined Cadet Force would be provided for separately. Although the formula by which the grant is calculated has changed from time to time, the system of subsidy from the States has remained more or less the same for more than 50 years.

When the College, post-war, reopened for business, school numbers increased rapidly, so much so that for the first time since the re-chartering, the main building was becoming overcrowded and additional premises were needed. A former nursing home, Beechwood, in Queen's Road, was identified as a suitable place to house the Lower School, freeing up valuable classroom space in the main building in the Grange. Beechwood had also once been the home of Sir William Carey (1477), Bailiff of Guernsey, 1908–1915.

Left: The College's Queen's Scouts meet the Queen.

Above: The badge of the College 'Pioneers', a group which existed alongside but was separate from the Scouts.

Below: Visit of the Chief Scout, Lord Rowallan, in 1954, accompanied here by WWM Cooper.

College Scouts

In 1908, the year Lord Baden-Powell published his *Scouting for Boys,* four young Elizabethans established the first Scout Group in Guernsey – AS Matthews (3018), WDM Lovell (3019), TO Guilbert (2983) and FL Howitt (3120) formed the Peewit Patrol. Although there were some fits and starts in the early days, a College troop, the 15th Guernsey, was in existence by 1927 but was short-lived. The present College Troop, 6th Guernsey, was set up in 1940. Although there were Scout-like activities when the College was in exile in Derbyshire, the troop was re-established only after the war when, under WWM Cooper (Coop), the Classics Master, the 6th Guernsey achieved remarkable results: in the late 1950s, there were more 'Queen's Scouts' at Elizabeth College than in any other school in Britain and the Queen herself inspected them on her visit in 1957. Fifteen members of the 6th attended the World Scout Jamboree in Holland in 1995, a record for Guernsey and unmatched by any other UK group.

The Rockmount Hotel, Cobo, where rough seas were often an added excitement during lunch.

In September 1948, however, the conversion of the building was way behind schedule. Arrangements were hurriedly made to accommodate the youngest two classes of the Lower School, Div ii and Div iii, in large rooms behind St John's Hostel at Saumarez Park. A taxing time for the staff, it was an exciting start to real school for the boys, aged seven and eight. At playtime, they had the whole of Saumarez Park at their disposal, including two football pitches. With no catering facilities on hand, lunch became an adventure in itself. The Rockmount Hotel at Cobo Bay agreed to feed the 50 boys and staff, and every day they

Beechwood House today; and, right, Beechwood Huts, 1968.

walked, crocodile fashion, to and from the hotel, a two-mile round trip. The Rockmount's owner, Bert Curr, organised a special Christmas Party for the boys at the end of term.

By the end of January 1949, the Beechwood nursing home was finally transformed into a bright new school with, even in those days of austerity, planned colour schemes, polished wood floors and blue and green framed blackboards. There had been a Lower School since the re-chartering of the College, but this was a new beginning for the department. It was lucky to have Major WCF Caldwell still in charge – a man with a good deal of old-fashioned experience, equal measures of military authority and common kindness. Crucially, he had already been with the College for nearly 30 years and was well aware of all the nuances of an island community.

There was another addition to College buildings at this time, a new squash court in the former Lower School playground. The gift of OEs and friends of the College, in memory of EB Waite (a master and Vice-Principal for 34 years), it was the first squash court in the island.

The 1950s saw further expansion with the acquisition of the Grange Club in Upland Road. The building provided

much-needed sixth form classrooms: a large downstairs room, formerly used for billiards and snooker, was ideal for a library and for sixth form private study periods. Two temporary huts were also erected south of the gym to provide additional science classrooms, particularly for junior forms. As with many temporary buildings, the huts became semi-permanent: when their use as classrooms came to an end, they were adapted as offices for the bursar and the Principal.

Squash

The new College court created such an interest that Guernsey later became a world centre of squash, in no small measure down to the training efforts of Reg Harbour, a College Maths master in the early 1970s. Among Harbour's champions were John Le Lievre (5926), who ranked fourth in England, his brother Richard (6251), an English champion while still at school, and Mark Roberts (6718), who achieved legendary status in Channel Island squash circles. Before all of them, the indomitable Max Trouteaud (4760), still playing in his 70s. With other island youngsters wanting to emulate their success, demand for courts outstripped supply and four more were built in King's Road, near the College playing fields but independent of the school. Guernsey then fostered further champions such as Lisa Opie and Martine Le Moignan, all trained by Harbour at King's Road. More recently, Chris Simpson (9153) represented Guernsey at the Manchester 2002, Melbourne 2006 and Delhi 2010 Commonwealth Games. He was European Junior Champion in 2006 and the British Under 23 Champion in 2009, having held several other junior national titles.

The 1957 Squash Team: MJ English (4738), SJ Hollyer-Hill (4857), SP Heyworth (4748), RCM Johnson (4550), RD Self (4959).

There was pressure on space, too, at the College Field. The OE Association acquired land at Footes Lane, which became a sports field in memory of OEs killed in World War II. Over the years, surrounding land was acquired and sports pitches at the Memorial Field now double up on those at the College Field.

Luck came the way of the College when the building known as the 'People's Palace' in Rue des Frères came on the market. Also known as Billy Bartlett's or the Flea Pit, it had been an early Guernsey cinema and occupied a site which formed part of the original friary lands granted to the College by Elizabeth I. With the help of a grant from the Industrial Fund, a magnificent new Science block was built, later to be named after Henry Milnes. The whole project had been, for him, a dream fulfilled, although, sadly, he never saw the finished building.

Below left: The Grange Club in the early twentieth century. It now houses the Modern Foreign Languages department.

Below: Aerial view, 1962.

The Milnes building, 1958,
and a Physics laboratory.

Milnes did, however, end his 18 years at the College on what was a moment of glory. On the last day of the summer term in 1957, the Queen and Prince Philip paid a visit to the College. Her Majesty inspected a CCF Guard of Honour, met Queen's Scouts assembled at the foot of the College steps and then signed the visitors' book in the Hall. She also admired the remarkable collection of silver trophies the Shooting VIII had brought home from Bisley on the mailboat that very morning.

It could not have been a prouder moment for Milnes. Only days later, beginning the school holidays in England, he fell seriously ill and was never able to return to Guernsey. He died in 1962, shortly after being awarded the OBE.

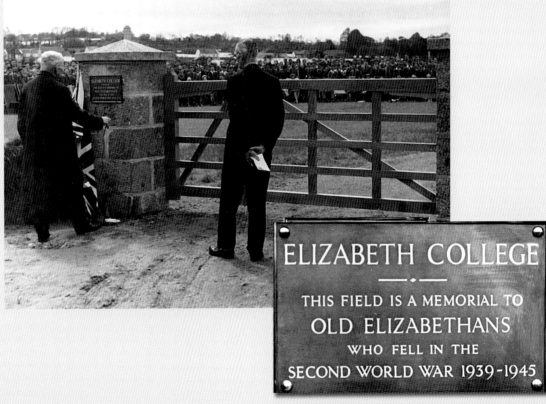

ELIZABETH COLLEGE

THIS FIELD IS A MEMORIAL TO
OLD ELIZABETHANS
WHO FELL IN THE
SECOND WORLD WAR 1939-1945

13

THE SWINGING SIXTIES

'The States of Guernsey have provided this fine building and many others. It is proper that Your Majesty should know that without the generosity of the States ... we could not be the school we are.'

ADDRESS TO HM THE QUEEN MOTHER BY THE SENIOR PREFECT, MAY 1963

'The College is not very popular with the island's Anglican rectors because we nick, as they see it, their choristers and confirmation candidates.'

JK DAY, IN A LETTER TO THE REVD PETER LANE, CANDIDATE FOR THE COLLEGE CHAPLAINCY

ENRY MILNES WAS a strict disciplinarian. In his later years as Principal, many boys considered him the most frightening and authoritarian man they had ever met. That may have been what parents wanted and expected of a headmaster in the 1930s and 1940s, but in the late 1950s it was out of tune with the changing attitudes of young people. Milnes was astounded when he was faced with a rebellion of the senior school refusing to do compulsory PT in their break time. Uncharacteristically, he backed down and the PT sessions were cancelled.

School assemblies and other events are held at St James. It has played a significant part in College life for nearly two centuries.

Above: Portrait of JK Day from the Le Marchant Room Collection.

Left: The Westcoasters, a hugely successful band formed by Elizabethans in the 1960s. From left to right: Jerry Girard (5442), Dave Fuller (4986), Neil Spensley (5606), Richard Paine (5062), Andy Fuller (5290).

Discipline was everything: correct personal appearance meant hands out of pockets, shirts tucked in, socks pulled up and short, combed hair. Boys should run when they were meant to run and walk when they were meant to walk, with no allowance for confusing the two. The only newspaper allowed was *The Times* — other newspapers were 'rags'.

That said, Milnes had his loyal followers, not only among the staff but among parents, too. For them, any choice of a successor would probably have been the wrong choice.

Hostility towards the appointment of JK Day, therefore, was a foregone conclusion. There were grumblings, too, that the College, for the first time, had a Principal who was not an ordained member of the Church of England. However, although Day lacked the domineering presence of his predecessor, he was broad-minded and genial and boys warmed to him. Not that he was against discipline — early on, he had given senior boys a pep talk on the dangers of smoking and reminded them of the College rules about doing so in public. Within half an hour, one of them was seen smoking in town: he was expelled.

JK Day and his family were not strangers to the island, nor, indeed, to the College. Mrs Day, Betty, had been born in the island when her father, Tom Stinton, was a College Classics master in the four years before the Great War. It was Stinton who had later encouraged his son-in-law to apply for the job in Guernsey. Day ('Jake' to the boys and 'Jan' to his friends and family) set about raising the academic

standards of the College to a point where its results would be comparable to a similar establishment on the mainland. It meant restructuring the entire system of classes, dividing forms into sets.

In his first Speech Day report in July 1958, Jan Day paid a handsome tribute to Henry Milnes but said, in effect, that only foundations for success had been laid and the real work lay ahead. He apologised for the poor academic results of the preceding year: 'We have won no Open Scholarships,

Right and below: Visit of HM the Queen Mother, 1963. HM was presented with a Tudor Rose by Nigel de la Rue (5841).

no Closed Scholarships, and no Exhibitions at the Universities: we have no scholar of the year to present … we have no one this year going to Oxford or Cambridge.'

By 1960, it was a happy Principal who addressed boys and parents at Speech Day. The new Science block, opened by the Vice-Chancellor of Southampton University, was fully functional and Day could announce that GCE passes at A and O level were much higher than they had been in previous years and three boys were going to Oxbridge, two as scholars. What particularly pleased Day was that PWM Cogman (4812), RP Giffard (4758) and IN McCave (4833) were the first to have come up the school from the age of seven at Beechwood — and they were natives of Guernsey,

too. They all gained First Class Honours degrees – McCave became a Cambridge professor, Giffard a professor at Stanford University, USA, and Cogman a senior lecturer at Southampton University.

At the invitation of the Principal and the Board of Directors, the College received a visit from UK Inspectors in October 1960. The HMIs noted the Principal had brought 'great sincerity of purpose and tactful calm to the task confronting him' in the matter of academic standards, but acknowledged the constant problems presented by 'an imposing but undoubtedly worrying building'. In addition to all the inadequacies that had been of everlasting concern, dry rot was discovered at Beechwood, in the Library Block, the Ozanne Building and the four turrets of the main building. 'If only someone could devise a means of preventing dry rot in Guernsey, this College would be a great deal cheaper to run', Day told a Speech Day audience.

In 1963, the school celebrated the quatercentenary of its foundation, the highlight of which was the visit of Queen Elizabeth the Queen Mother. The Senior Prefect, PV Sarre (4988), welcomed Her Majesty on 10 May 'on behalf of 400 years of pupils' and continued an address which was clearly meant to be heard by Guernsey politicians.

> We have solid as well as sentimental cause for gratitude to Your Majesty's namesake, our Foundress. And not only to our Royal Foundress, but many later benefactors … chief among these, the States of Guernsey have provided this fine building and many others …paying the College a generous direct grant and the fees of a large number of our pupils. It is proper that Your Majesty should know that without the generosity of the States … we could not be the school we are.

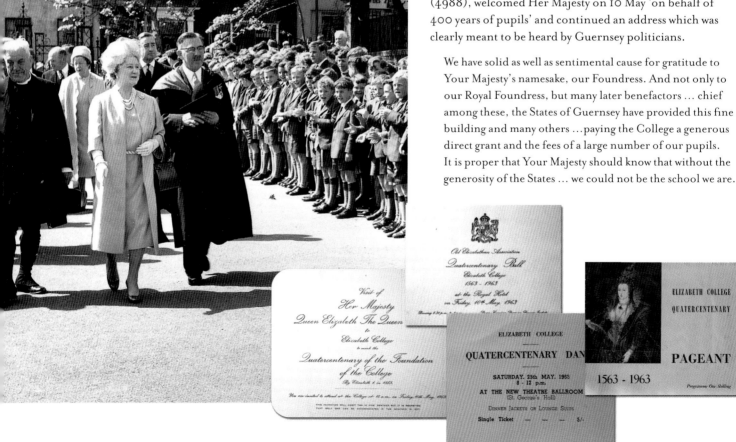

Francis Hockaday was porter for many years.

Unsung heroes

Since 1824, the College has employed a colourful collection of non-teaching staff – school porters such as Francis Hockaday, introduced to King George V in 1921, and Nicholson, in the nineteenth century. When presented with a meerschaum tobacco pipe on his retirement, Nicholson was so overcome that he spluttered out a request for a school holiday and it was immediately granted by Principal Bromby. Nicholson allowed Amias Andros (878) to toll the long-disappeared great College bell, 'a pleasure only those who have shared in it can possibly appreciate. That bell which brings the youth of Guernsey scampering down the Grange takes some pulling; and I for one threw my whole soul into it. You caught hold of the rope and it lifted you off your legs – Ding! Dong! went the bell and then up you went to the ceiling'.

For longevity, however, none can match the groundsman, Bill Allen. Starting work at the College Field in 1902, he retired when he was 80 in 1967. Short-tempered and sharp-featured, he was a legendary figure. During the German occupation he risked imprisonment by helping two OE army officers, on a spying mission, escape detection by hiding them in the pavilion. Lt HF Nicolle (4193) and Lt JM Symes (3967) had been unable to leave the island at the appointed time – they eventually surrendered to the authorities and were sent to German prison camps. Lt P Martel (3673) and Lt JD Mulholland (4037) were also sent to Germany after similar reconnaissance landings. All four were awarded the Military Cross.

Bill Allen.

The Queen Mother was presented with a silver brooch in the form of the Tudor Arms and an Elizabethan rose which she immediately pinned to her coat.

Considerable time and effort were spent during the 1960s trying to work out a suitable future relationship between the College and St James's Church. The College Hall was no longer big enough for the whole school to attend any kind of assembly together and Day was keen to take over the former garrison church on a permanent basis. With a dwindling parish congregation and mounting repair bills, the Trustees of St James were equally keen. However, the daily use of St James as a chapel and, more particularly, as a parish church on Sundays had caused tensions within the island's Anglican hierarchy for a number of years. Parish rectors saw choristers and confirmation candidates enticed away to St James from their own congregations. The Rector of St Martin's, the Revd FW Cogman, was particularly upset with Day when his own senior chorister became head of the College choir and defected to St James. The matter was clearly not forgotten when Cogman later became Dean of Guernsey and *ex-officio* Chairman of the Directors. The stand-off between Cogman and Day faded for a while when the States Engineer ruled St James structurally unsafe to use.

The whole issue was reignited, however, when Day decided the best candidate for a new school chaplain was a Methodist minister, the Revd Peter Lane. Cogman demanded the intervention of the Bishop of Winchester, Dr Falkner Allison, who hinted that 'the appointment of a Methodist Chaplain in a school with a very strong Anglican tradition … might well create more problems than it solved'.

A plaque is unveiled by the Lt Governor, Sir Alexander Boswell, to commemorate Hubert Nicolle and Jim Symes hiding from German forces in the pavilion. (See above). Inset: Nicolle as a prisoner of war.

Cogman was more forthright: 'I have been placed in a position where I am likely to be at variance with the rest of the Island clergy through no fault of my own and I am not prepared to be a means of causing division and discontent among my brethren of the clergy.'

The truth is that the problem was not so much an inter-denominational squabble but more the concern that St James might once again reopen as a successful parish church in its own right. It was a painful moment for the College and especially for Jan Day, deeply religious and unsuited to petty squabbles. Nobody won the argument – Peter Lane was appointed, but St James fell into further decay and was never again used for regular worship. Subsequent attempts to have the church demolished were overturned by a well-organised campaign and St James is now an island assembly and concert hall, but is still used for weekly College assemblies. Peter Lane had a successful career at the College and was later elected a Jurat of the Royal Court, one of the island's highest honours.

The row over St James may have hastened Jan Day's retirement, but his place in College history was already secure. The Milnes Laboratories, the Winchester Building, the refitting of the Ozanne Building, Beechwood upgraded, all had been completed during his 14 years in office. In his last summer term, Day's list of Oxbridge entrants was a testimony to what he had set out to achieve in his teaching reforms. *Oxford*: a scholarship in Physics at Exeter; two places at Pembroke, one an open scholarship in Engineering and an Exhibition in Engineering Science at Jesus. *Cambridge*: two places at Emmanuel, one an Open Exhibition in General Studies and a place at Fitzwilliam.

Both St James and the main College building appear on Guernsey banknotes – St James on the £20 note and the College, below, on the £10 note.

It would be wrong to leave any impression that Day had concentrated solely on raising the academic status of the College to the exclusion of other areas of school life. Far from it. Games flourished, so did the CCF, shooting and the school's many other outside activities. For the record, the Day era ushered in two sartorial changes — coloured house ties were introduced and caps were no longer to be worn by members of the senior school.

The College chaplain in the 1960s, the Revd Alan Charters, went on to become headmaster of Gloucester Cathedral Choir School. Paying tribute to Jan Day at his memorial service — in St James — Charters had this to say:

> As College Principal it must have been difficult for him to follow his passionate conviction that we were not doing enough for the deprived. One of my abiding memories is of him, when school was over, going out in his old duffle coat with his Labrador, Humphrey Beamish, delivering Oxfam envelopes in all parts of the island with very little support. As lay reader in charge of the local church in Norfolk, he could be found sweeping it out in preparation for Sunday worship. No job worth doing was beneath his dignity, no human being ever attracted his contempt.

James Burge (5724) was at Elizabeth College throughout the 1960s and became a producer of television documentaries and an accomplished author. His father, Colonel Bill Burge, was a popular Maths master. James recalls some of the Colonel's colleagues, all on the staff from the 1940s to the 1970s.

> In retrospect I realise that, at its heart, Elizabeth College itself was rooted in the pre-war world. The educational ethos of the school was represented by a core of veteran schoolmasters whose eccentricities were varied, but what they all had in common is that they flew rather satisfyingly in the face of modern educational best practice.
>
> Mr Cooper taught Latin. His Brillo-pad grey hair and stooped gait might have earned the epithet doddery, but a wiry frame that suggested a tendency for hiking and exercise was borne out by his headship of the school scout troop.

Above: The College photograph of 1965.

Left: James Burge.

> He drummed into our heads the supine of confiteor ('confisu', since you ask) and gave the time-honoured answer to the question, 'Please Sir, why do we have to learn Latin?' (it trains the mind). He prefaced the O-level Latin course with a speech to the effect that it was his intention to lay out the knowledge and if we cared to absorb it we stood every chance of getting an O-level, but he would make no effort beyond that.
>
> Mr van Leuven ('Vandy') taught English which consisted of extraordinarily dull exercises in comprehension and occasional group performances of the odd scene from Shakespeare. Just occasionally, he would give the iconic performance on which his reputation as an eccentric really rested. He would seize the board rubber — a block of wood about six inches in length to which felt was attached — and hurl it across the classroom at some recalcitrant pupil with a shriek of 'Pay attention boyeee!'. Although this hard missile had the potential to injure, he seemed to have enough skill to miss the target. I never heard of any injuries, not even in the annals of schoolboy lore. These days he would certainly lose his job and find himself in court for such behaviour.

Micky Manchester taught History. I found his lessons, which consisted entirely of talk, boring, the unacceptable face of the old guard. But now, far too late, I owe him an apology. I have spent much of my life making television programmes about history. Whenever I encounter a new period about which I know little, lodged in my memory are the key facts and very often the quotes which I need to tell the story. These vital nuggets were put there against my will during the boredom of Micky's lessons. He plainly had a great gift for history which I had been very foolishly resisting.

Mr Nixon taught French. He had more claim than most to represent the official culture of the British ruling class since he had been to Eton. He was a stickler for correct pronunciation: nonetheless he managed always to sound like an Englishman pronouncing French well. On cold winter days, he would insist on opening the classroom windows. Pupils could see above the belt of his trousers the tops of pyjama bottoms, worn underneath to protect him from the cold. He would walk up and down, jangling loose change in his pocket, analysing the plot of Corneille's 'Le Cid'. He extemporised translations of the dialogue in the language of his student days: 'Come along, gal!', 'I say, well done!' or 'I'll bid you good day, Sir!', making the characters sound like refugees from the works of that great OE, PG Wodehouse.

Nixon's other claim to fame was his presence in the *Guinness Book of Records*. Since Cambridge he had held the British ski-jump distance record. He had made a very long jump, but what kept him in the record book was that the rules had changed shortly afterwards and marks were awarded for style as well as distance. No Brit subsequently bothered to make such a long and ungainly flight until the 1990s, when Nixon's record was finally broken by another great English eccentric known as Eddie the Eagle.

Some of the masters were younger and arrived fresh-faced during my time at the school, treating their pupils as if they were members of the same species. One in particular had an understanding of the new element in our lives: the media. He was also a writer and BBC broadcaster. He took his pupils on a tour of the *Guernsey Press*, where I had the privilege of witnessing the historic printing presses and hot metal process when it was still the centre of journalism. His good humour and encouragement have not been forgotten by any of his pupils, least of all by me. He founded a junior newspaper and even gave the unbearably bolshie younger me a chance to be on the editorial board. He went on to make a career in television until, eventually, life brought him full circle to author this book.

Van Leuven.   Micky Manchester.

MUSICAL TIMES

*'Elizabeth College is an amazingly busy
school with a range of opportunities
which would do credit to a school of
more than twice its size.'*

<small>RICHARD WHEADON, PRINCIPAL</small>

ONE OF RICHARD WHEADON'S first thoughts, when
he became Principal in 1972, was that the main
buildings were not fit for purpose and the College
should be moved to a more suitable site, possibly adjacent to
the College field. He was unaware that the Board of
Education Inspectors had come to exactly the same
conclusion in 1920 when the school was much smaller.

While the idea had been virtually ignored by the island
half a century previously, Wheadon was surprised and
delighted when his suggestion was met 'with unanimous
agreement and enthusiasm'. For the following five years, the
Directors looked at possible sites, including Vimiera in the
Rohais, Meadow View in Footes Lane and Springfield in
Queen's Road. Initially, the States of Guernsey planning
department (IDC) was comfortable with the idea of

Left: Choir in St Brieuc, 1967.

Inset: School House badge.

Below: Choir and orchestra.

transplanting the College to a more spacious site and the planning officer, Sylvester White, readily engaged with the Directors in their search. Although known for his aversion to change, Major Tom Ogier (3603), IDC President, had commissioned a feasibility report. When he read it, however, he went cold on the whole idea and that was the end of the matter.

The discussions in the 1970s did, at least, lead the Directors to look for other solutions. The consequent decision to construct a new boarding house in King's Road,

Portrait of Richard Wheadon
from the Le Marchant Room
Collection.

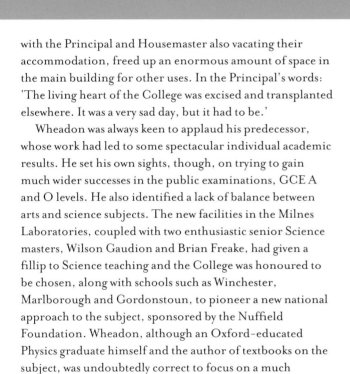

Carmen Elizabethanum

Verse 1
In antiqua insula
Stat praeclarum fanum,
Litteris, scientiis,
Elizabethanum

Verse 2
Sarnia carissima,
Floreas, florebis,
Litteris, scientiis,
Numquam indigebis.

Verse 3
Caro in Collegio
Multa nos docemur,
Colimus praecipue
Fidem qua fovemur

Verse 4
Fundatricis memores
Virginis reginae,
Cujus vita dedita est
Fidei Divinae.

Chorus
Corpus sic coniungimus
Menti sanae sanum
Floret sic collegium
Elizabethanum.

Left: The School Song.

Below: Foundress's Day
service in the Town
Church.

with the Principal and Housemaster also vacating their
accommodation, freed up an enormous amount of space in
the main building for other uses. In the Principal's words:
'The living heart of the College was excised and transplanted
elsewhere. It was a very sad day, but it had to be.'

Wheadon was always keen to applaud his predecessor,
whose work had led to some spectacular individual academic
results. He set his own sights, though, on trying to gain
much wider successes in the public examinations, GCE A
and O levels. He also identified a lack of balance between
arts and science subjects. The new facilities in the Milnes
Laboratories, coupled with two enthusiastic senior Science
masters, Wilson Gaudion and Brian Freake, had given a
fillip to Science teaching and the College was honoured to
be chosen, along with schools such as Winchester,
Marlborough and Gordonstoun, to pioneer a new national
approach to the subject, sponsored by the Nuffield
Foundation. Wheadon, although an Oxford-educated
Physics graduate himself and the author of textbooks on the
subject, was undoubtedly correct to focus on a much
increased emphasis and, therefore, achievement in arts and
the humanities. He arrived in Guernsey with a string of
musical credits behind him, both choral and instrumental.
At Oxford he sang in the city's Bach Choir; as a master at
Eton and at Dauntsey's he played principal horn in both
school orchestras.

At Elizabeth College there was already some musical
expertise, but it was limited. With weekly practices for parish
services at St James and a former King's College,
Cambridge, choral scholar as its conductor, the school
choir under Eric Waddams had been renowned for its fine
performances and made regular BBC radio broadcasts.
Choir trips to Brittany began in 1967, with 'Les Petits

Music Technology.

Chanteurs de Guernesey' charming their concert audiences in any number of cathedral cities of northern France. One of the highlights of the choir year is still the annual visit of more than 50 boys to St Malo. A special anthem was performed in the town's cathedral to commemorate the 40th anniversary of the choir trips, the Latin words written by Alan Cross, Director of Studies, and the music composed by Peter Harris, Director of Music.

Notwithstanding this choral success, the College, in the 1970s, was lagging behind in the teaching of music generally, along with other island schools. There was a concentration on keyboard and choral, and any school instrumentalists of note had been taught privately. When Waddams retired, Richard Wheadon appointed a violinist, Miles Attwell, as Director of Music. 'I knew that if I had a violinist, he would grow an orchestra.' A year later, the new post of Director of Choral Music was created. When choosing other subject masters, Wheadon also made a point of looking favourably on those with musical skills. The school soon had a junior and a senior orchestra and then a wind band. The Elizabeth College Summer Orchestral Course was created and regularly attracts nearly 300 students, not just from the Channel Islands but from the UK and the rest of Europe.

The music department now has a profusion of computers in its technology suite, allowing students to approach composition according to their particular abilities. The general improvement in the teaching and performance of music at the College, together with a similar step forward at the Ladies' College, had a broadening effect on music throughout Guernsey. John Stephenson of the States Education Department, a former English master at the College, was instrumental in the appointment of an Island Director of Music and the establishment of a Schools' Music Service to cater for all levels of young Guernsey musicians. In later years, the Gibson Fleming Trustees decided to award extra scholarships for music at the College.

The 1970s and 1980s were generally good for sport – the Principal was an Oxford rowing blue and a Great Britain

M de Figueiredo and BJ Richardson scored centuries against Victoria College, 1968.

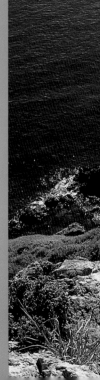

Alan Cross,
Director of Studies,
1994–2009.

oarsman in the 1956 Olympics, so games were hardly likely to be neglected – the majority of cricket, football and athletics matches against Victoria College were won by Elizabeth.

Richard Wheadon gave his own account of his time as Principal in his foreword to Keith Bichard's Volume IV of the *College Register*. The College had come a long way in the preceding four decades, he wrote, and in his final year it boasted an A level pass rate of 95.6 per cent. 'Elizabeth College is an amazingly busy school with a range of opportunities which would do credit to a school of more than twice its size.'

Wheadon's successor, John Doulton, however, found a school whose 'human face and public image needed attention'. While Doulton saluted Richard Wheadon's insistence on aiming for high standards, he perceived that in the process 'Elizabeth College had acquired a reputation for being somewhat arrogant and authoritarian. Staff had become discouraged from expressing opinions … parents were nervous that little understanding would be shown when their sons' behaviour was less than perfect'.

If the age of deference had died off in the English public school system, it was still alive in Guernsey. Richard Wheadon's staff were referred to as *under*-masters, a term

resurrected from the nineteenth century. He insists that, according to the statutes, this was their legal definition and he used it only when drawing up their contracts. However, they all had to call him 'Sir' and, off duty or not, they were expected to stand up when he came into a room. While many parents might have applauded such an old-fashioned approach to good manners, many of the staff regarded it as outmoded and demeaning.

Alan Cross, who later became Director of Studies, was one of Wheadon's appointees. He says the teaching staff, including the Vice-Principal (Vernon Collenette, who had been a master since 1948), were very definitely expected to remember that they were Wheadon's subordinates, but he finds no fault with his commitment to the fortunes of the College in all areas of its life.

He was a strong supporter of the CCF, for example, and loved to be associated with the ceremonial occasions, Remembrance Day, royal visits, and so on. On these and all public occasions, his turn-out was pristine, immaculate. The last of the truly old-style Principals – he may have quickly eschewed beatings – but just behind the velvet was always the hint of steel.

Duke of Edinburgh's Award

The Duke of Edinburgh's Award Scheme, operating partly through the aegis of the CCF, became increasingly popular from its introduction in the 1960s; the late 1990s were especially successful, with eight members of the College achieving the gold standard.

Climbing, mountaineering, coasteering and other pursuits, once loosely labelled as 'arduous training', became important activities under the CCF umbrella and included a wide variety of other activities such as abseiling, lifesaving, gliding and orienteering.

Many took the challenge of walking and mountaineering expeditions to Dartmoor, the Lake District and further afield, with fierce competition for places on events such as the annual Ten Tors challenge or adventure training in the, often snow-bound, Cairngorms. Kayak Camps, the biggest of which have been held on Herm Common, involved boys bivouacking on the island after kayaking across the Little Russel.

Expeditions have been organised to Greece, Poland, Corsica and the French Alps.

15

HELLO GIRLS

'My best qualities come from my time at Elizabeth College, and I wouldn't change a single one. As do some of my best friendships. We went where no other woman has gone before — and that's not easy to say in an all boys' public school.'

Zoe Ash, one of the first six girls to join the College in the 1990s

I N HIS EFFORTS TO reduce the perceived 'tension' in the school community, John Doulton sought the opinion of all members of the teaching staff in a full review of the workings of the College. The review quickly spawned the foundation of an association of parents and staff to organise social events. The 'Friends of the College' were also responsible for innumerable gifts of scientific, computing and printing equipment, new girdles for the choir, the refurbishment of honours boards and a computerised stage lighting system for the Hall. In reality, the Upper School was only catching up with what had been happening fairly successfully for some time with parents, staff and support groups in the Lower School at Beechwood.

Beechwood itself, however, was being identified as in need of complete modernisation and there were moves to

College production of *Oliver*, 2008.

Beechwood in 1960 (left) and (right), modernised and enlarged in recent decades. Acorn House (below), once the boarding house, was converted into a school for infants and opened in 1996.

give it greater autonomy. Repeated arguments in the past over what powers and status the master in charge of Beechwood should enjoy were finally put to rest when he was accorded the title 'Headteacher' and allowed a freer rein over how the school was run. Although Beechwood as a separate entity was formally acknowledged, it was still to be the ultimate responsibility of the Directors and the Principal. A slightly unexpected result of this increased independence, but much welcomed nevertheless, was greater co-operation between Beechwood and the Upper School, especially in drama and music. As the standard of music at Beechwood improved, junior school boys became a regular feature in Upper School musical events. A notable production was *Noah and his Floating Zoo* in 1994 when Beechwood's headteacher, the popular David Williams, marked his retirement from Beechwood by singing the part of God. He became a school inspector.

Even though the boarders had moved out of their substandard accommodation in the Grange for new premises at King's Road, the improvement was not enough to attract extra entrants: in common with other schools on the mainland, the College boarding house fell victim to

Portrait of John Doulton from the Le Marchant Room Collection.

changing attitudes on the part of parents and a decline in the number of children being sent away to board. For a school in the Channel Islands, the problem was exacerbated by increasingly high fares on air and sea routes from the mainland. Numbers declined to a point where it was not financially viable to keep the boarding house open.

The gradual demise of the boarding house proved, with hindsight, a cloud with a silver lining. In 1995, a growing requirement for independent infant schooling in Guernsey led to discussions about how the need might be met by using the surplus boarding accommodation now available at King's Road. An immediate advantage was the existing availability of facilities to provide cooked lunches for the infants as well as older boys at Beechwood. A fairly modest building programme was all that was needed to make a viable infant school: construction went ahead and the wife of the Lt Governor, Lady Coward, officially opened Acorn House in October 1996.

'It was a nervous moment owing to the shortage of pupils', according to John Doulton, 'but fears rapidly proved to be unfounded. The school flourished, in no small part due to the clarity, warmth and energy of Mrs Beryl Amy's leadership.' Indeed, the time was not far off when demand for places would outstrip supply.

John Doulton maintains that over a period of time under his direction, the College had become a more relaxed institution without losing its insistence on high standards. Some staff at the College were concerned, however, about competition from the Grammar School and they considered pupil numbers were being kept up by lowering the standard of entry. Added to that, boys who struggled

A *Guernsey Press* cartoonist appears bemused by the arrival of a group of girls at the College.

academically were being allowed to remain at the school if there was anything else they might contribute to the community such as sporting prowess. In the words of one former member of staff: 'Perhaps inadvertently, John contributed to the image of the College as an old-fashioned, provincial public school.'

September 1992 saw an historic moment when the College welcomed a group of girls into the sixth form from a relocating Blanchelande College. Although not the only girls to have attended classes – Carolyn Mauger of the Ladies'

First intake

Zoe Ash (8993) was one of the 'Blanchelande six' to enrol at the College. She made journalism her career and joined the *Guernsey Press* as a reporter:

Plucked from an all-girls convent school, we were dropped into the entirely testosterone-fuelled world that was Elizabeth College. At 15, I had lived in an entirely female world, forbidden to board the school bus home unless properly dressed, white gloves and all. But our world was turned upside down when, in our GCSE year, Blanchelande College, since reopened, was earmarked for closure.

Out-numbered by ten to one in our year and a hundred to one in the whole College, the words 'and ladies' were hastily hand-written on all the literature handed to my parents, and separate toilets and a common room allocated. Suddenly we were in a world where you were called by your surname, and known by your number – something more mysterious and secretive than the Da Vinci Code itself. You would not have to be a code breaker to gain access to any OE's bank account …

Our skirts were to be strictly below the knee and College rules (for boys) stated hair should not touch the shirt collar – one that thankfully did not apply to us. You could only take off your blazer and tie and undo your top button if a sign was posted in the College Hall – and temperatures generally had to be over 90 degrees for this to happen.

In the Upper Sixth, we were integrated into the main common room, albeit in the kitchen – some clichés are just too easy. The odd love letter was dropped into blazer pockets and I'm sure we probably caused more sparks to fly than usual on College trips.

There were times when I'm not sure they knew what to do with us. The boys did CCF, we were sent to Beau Séjour for aerobics. Our short tennis skirts caused a stir and the fact we only had to do two, not three laps of the cross-country course incited a petition. But we were smart girls, and not fazed. While Blanchelande had religiously taught us to work hard,

Elizabeth College matched that with the life skills that taught us to play hard, too. And always fair.

We are the first female student faces in the Elizabeth College school photographs and are the first female names engraved on the trophies. Something time, and no man, can change. Men who were young boys when we breezed up those fine front steps talk of the buzz of girls being there but we were, thankfully, oblivious at the time. Taking the untrodden path to Elizabeth College undoubtedly changed my life. It gave me a unique identity that I have carried with me ever since. A sense of confidence and courage that can only come from fighting for your right to be where you are. My best qualities come from my time at Elizabeth College as do some of my best friendships. We went where no other woman has gone before – and that's not easy to say in an all boys' public school. And like most OEs, my College number will be indelibly imprinted on my proud heart for ever – but definitely not on my bank account.

Country House Sixth Form, 1995.

College blazed a trail by taking a chemistry A level in the 1950s – the six Blanchelande students were the first girls to be officially registered with those cherished school numbers.

The entry of the Blanchelande girls provoked much discussion about possible future provision of mixed-sex classes and plans for co-operation between the island's secondary schools at this level. Several stumbling blocks ahead were identified, not least what any such liaison might do to the viability of the Ladies' College sixth form, and no formal agreement was reached. The whole issue resurfaced when Doulton's successor, David Toze, became Principal.

A complete refurbishment of the science laboratories, the transfer of the geography department to the former gymnasium and many other improvements were highlights of the Doulton era. The most significant addition to the College site was the new sports hall, opened by the Bailiff, Sir Charles Frossard, KBE (3929), in 1993, which hugely enhanced the facilities for sport and physical education. Indoor cricket nets, a climbing wall and space for table tennis were all features of the new complex. Another project was the demolition of age-old huts behind the gym to allow a purpose-built art department on the site.

At Beechwood, temporary classrooms which had taken on a permanent air were demolished and replaced by a building which housed four classrooms, Science laboratory, design and technology room, gym, hall, staff room, resources room, changing rooms and cloakrooms. More classrooms were added later. The new facilities were to transform Beechwood and, together with far-reaching staff changes in the following decade, provided the modernisation needed to meet the demands of increasingly discerning parents.

Although John Doulton was appointed on a ten-year contract, he might have expected an extension when it expired, a few years short of his 60th birthday, but the Directors were against any such renewal. In coming to this decision, they may well have been unfair, for when they met to discuss it, not one member of the Board could find any specific fault with Doulton's running of the school. The Directors felt, however, that after ten years, fresh blood was needed to drive the school ahead into the new millennium.

Doulton's verdict on this unexpected rebuff reveals one of the difficulties faced by the Principal of a high-profile school in a small island community – at least in the dying twentieth century, if not so much now. His wife, Margaret, found it difficult to establish a life for herself in the island where she always had to be 'the Principal's wife' and, for him, the need always to be 'a smiley face' in the island proved hard to cope with: 'At Radley College, I had been purposely given a house to run that rather prided itself on being the school's centre of non-achievement in almost every respect, as well as being a hotbed of indiscipline and bullying. I was given it because I was reckoned to be nasty enough and sufficiently bloody-minded to pull it out of the mire – and I did so. So it was odd to have to accept the reverse role!' Doulton admits that when it came to cracking the whip, as he had at Radley, he fell short of what might have been required in Guernsey. In the words of one senior Director, he was far too 'laid back'.

The Directors appointed a successor who was anything but laid back.

16

MILLENNIUM MAKEOVERS

'Some went off into dark corners, never fully to re-emerge, except to hand in their resignations.'

ALAN CROSS, DIRECTOR OF STUDIES, REACTING TO DAVID TOZE'S MISSION STATEMENT AFTER HIS APPOINTMENT AS PRINCIPAL

'*A*FTER TEN YEARS OF stressful and highly demanding school leadership, a stint at Elizabeth College would be a rest cure,' suggested the recruitment agency to David Toze. He agreed, attracted by the thought of a rest cure at that particular stage in his career, and took the job as Principal in 1998. At the age of 46, he had already been Principal of the American Community School in Surrey, Rector of the Anglo-Colombian School in Bogota and Director of the Vienna International School.

For a month, Toze held in check his self-acknowledged 'hyper-active and driven personality' but then abandoned the promised rest cure and got down to business. Alan Cross welcomed him as a reforming genius: 'From his broad international perspective, he saw the College as a moribund

institution in a mentally and culturally insular community, and lost no time in setting about bringing it, kicking and screaming, into the modern educational world.'

Toze himself has set out what he discerned as the College problems that needed dealing with quickly: 'The structure of Guernsey's secondary education was in the middle of a fundamental review; the financial grant that underpinned the College's revenue stream was in jeopardy; there was a move to try to consolidate all sixth form teaching in one place – the death knell by stealth of Elizabeth College, since it would decimate student numbers and discourage mainland teachers from applying to work there. I was generally concerned with the quality of teaching and learning. Good schools are built from the bottom up and not from the top down. The programme for the seven- to eleven-year-olds, particularly, was trapped in a time warp somewhere in the 1950s, with teacher-centred, content-driven, textbook-led lessons that discouraged inquiry-based learning in any form.'

Toze made significant changes in personnel. 'My fundamental belief is that schools exist to provide high quality education for children and not to provide jobs for teachers.'

One of his most eye-catching appointments was of Suzanne Battey to the headship of Beechwood – a strong leader in place where, by common accord, one was needed. She was also Beechwood's first woman headteacher.

She recalls that her appointment in 2000 caused raised eyebrows, especially in the Beechwood staff room where some had spent their whole teaching lives: 'We began the school year with seven new staff, new resources (we filled skip after skip of outdated materials and antiquated furniture) and a commitment to make Beechwood into a stimulating and flourishing environment for its pupils.'

The Dramatic Society was formed in 1891, became the Theatrical Society in 1910 and subsequently the Shakespearean Society. Today, College drama is more adventurous, with spectacular productions of plays and musicals such as *The Wizard of Oz* (above) and *Journey's End* (right).

Andy Priaulx

AG (Andy) Priaulx (8109), who was World Touring Car champion for three years running, started his motor racing career at the age of eight, karting in Guernsey. Before reaching world championship status in circuit racing, Andy had contented himself with hillclimbing and took the British Hillclimb Championship in 1995. In Guernsey that year, he competed in the same Val des Terres championship as his father, GE Priaulx (5507), who came seventh to his son's fourth. GE Priaulx's two brothers were both at the College, as was their father, EA Priaulx (4017), and his three brothers. Careers in engineering have spanned all three Priaulx generations.

Although slightly daunted by the arrival of a team of inspectors seven weeks into the new term, her anxiety was misplaced. The report could hardly have been better: 'Beechwood is a good school. The quality of leadership and teaching is good, as is the positive reinforcement of behaviour and work.'

Suzanne Battey remains uncompromising in her praise for David Toze, 'a mover and shaker in everything that happened … an inspirational colleague who empowered me to develop the school into what it is today … a huge shock when he announced his resignation'.

In the ten years that followed, Acorn House and Beechwood merged into one school with 45 per cent more pupils – girls remaining in the system until the age of 11. The buildings were extended and virtually given a complete facelift.

In the Senior School, Rick James, then Head of English and the sixth form, while admitting that Toze was divisive with his wholesale reorganisation, found him stimulating to work with and dynamic in the classroom: 'He questioned everything, an uncomfortable experience for some teachers, and his style could be abrasive and confrontational. He pursued the sixth form link with the Ladies' College, driving it forward when others would have taken rather more time. He always said that you don't manage change but lead it.' During the three, whirlwind years of the David Toze tenure as Principal, many were left dispirited by his far-reaching changes – some left without a job – others felt let down badly that he had packed it in so soon and not seen through the changes he had begun.

Fencing Academy

When the Elizabeth College Academy of Fencing was launched in 2010, it immediately became a blueprint for the regional provider of the newly founded British National Fencing Academy – the training ground for tomorrow's Olympians. There had been a fencing master on the staff as early as 1828 when Mons Alexandre Victor Marie Bourdic was appointed, but the post soon lapsed. It was only when Dr Robert Harnish joined the College in 2001 that fencing really came into its own. He decided to use the small fencing club (there were five athletes at the time) as a means of encouraging into sport those boys who did not enjoy the big three sports.

Dr Harnish soon thought the College was capable of winning the Public Schools' Fencing Championships – one of the largest amateur sporting events in Europe. In 2006, the College was the most improved school at the Championships and the following year also claimed the Bartlett Cup as the best boys' team in the country. In 2008, the College was the most improved school for the third year running – the first time such an achievement had been made in the long history of the competition; an achievement that is more remarkable as it was already the best school. It didn't stop there. In 2008, the cumulative points achieved by the College boys outstripped the sum of the boys' and girls' totals for top schools such as Brentwood and Millfield. That year, College fencers with an average age of 16½ years brought home a team bronze medal from the Commonwealth U20 Championships in Penang, Malaysia.

Portrait of Dr Nick Argent from the Le Marchant Room Collection.

Dr Nick Argent, who came to Guernsey from a job as the headmaster of a Northern Ireland grammar school, was well qualified to handle bruised egos and other sensitivities. Rick James, who was to become Vice-Principal, says Argent reunited the staff but was also able to build on Toze's reforms. 'Nick always acknowledged that David made things easier for him, but it took skill to settle the school and take it forward again.'

Argent had two perceived priorities for the College: to improve academic standards and encourage extra-curricular opportunities. His mastery of IT continued Toze's efforts to lift the College from one millennium to another.

The fencing team won eight trophies at the 2011 Public Schools' Fencing Championship.

Rifle shooting at Fort Le Marchant.

Elizabeth College Foundation

The Elizabeth College Foundation, a Guernsey and UK registered charity, was set up in 2006 to provide long-term financial stability, a luxury persistently denied to the school throughout its history. The Foundation has a set of objectives which include the provision of those additional enhancements which would not otherwise have been possible to fund out of general income: new buildings, improvements to existing facilities, bursaries, scholarships, as well as a wider aim of bringing together members of the Elizabeth College community.

The first Foundation venture was a very successful development appeal, under the chairmanship of Advocate RA Perrot (5450). Through the generosity of many OEs, parents and College supporters, this funded four desperately needed projects: a new sixth form centre, the Robin Roussel Pavilion, the Acorn House library and music room and the Beechwood all-weather pitch.

A thriving arm of the College Foundation is the Dead Donkey Club, membership of which is restricted to those OEs and College friends who have made provision for the school in their wills.

Cake commemorating the opening of the Robin Roussel Pavilion, 2010.

He breathed extra life into College hockey, taking personal charge of training and managing the 2nd XI — unbeaten against Jersey in his time at the College. He umpired cricket matches, took a huge interest in College shooting and always went to Bisley with the VIII.

'Nick Argent is rightly proud of the academic success achieved by Elizabeth College during his eight years as Principal', says Alan Cross, who retired as Director of Studies when Argent himself left. 'It is no coincidence that, given the bias of his own abilities and professional skills, the academic results improved year by year to their current very high level. Nick would rightly say it was a team effort, but the team recognised that without his encouragement and committed leadership, we might easily not have reached the standards which led to our being rated "outstanding" in so many areas of the 2009 Inspection report.'

The bonds between the College and the OE Association were also strengthened during Argent's time. G Barber (5159), the OEA Secretary at the time, says: 'As Principal, he always encouraged the OEA to be as involved as possible with College life. He put great importance, too, on making present Elizabethans aware of OEs and what they do for their old school.'

Dr Argent left the College in 2009 to become headmaster of Maidstone Grammar School. The end of the decade also saw the departure of a College stalwart, Stuart Morris, who had been on the staff for 37 years and, remarkably, Vice-Principal for 25 of them.

George Hartley, appointed Principal 2009, and family.

George Hartley took over as Principal after six years at Berkhamsted School as deputy headmaster.

In his first years at Elizabeth College, he has been keen to maintain respect for its historic traditions while, at the same time, developing and pushing it further into what he calls 'an exemplary, modern, independent school providing the best possible all-round educational experience in Guernsey'.

In the post-war decades, there have been both successes and failures. As might be expected, George Hartley is building on the successes with an increased emphasis on the merits of a broad education. With a firm focus on academic achievement, Principal Hartley also fervently underlines the importance today of sports, music, outdoor pursuits and other extra-curricular activities. Pupils are encouraged to broaden their horizons — not least by taking part in more than 100 off-island trips a year — but there is also a corresponding emphasis on giving something back to the island community in the form of public service.

His stewardship will, doubtless, begin the next history of an illustrious Elizabeth College.

Floreat Collegium!

4747

View of the college frontage from the Cochrane Map, 1832.

TIMELINE

1500s

1563 Foundation of Elizabeth College by Royal Charter (Letters Patent, 25 May 1563) and appointment of first Master, Dr Adrian Saravia (Statutes laid down 27 September)

1568 Second grant of adjoining land and house for use of College. The Governor hands over school property to Bailiff, Jurats and States of Guernsey, 'to belong for ever to the *Grande Ecole de notre Souveraine Dame Elizabeth Reine d'Angleterre*'

1590 Plague year – College building requisitioned for use as prison

College Statutes, 1563.

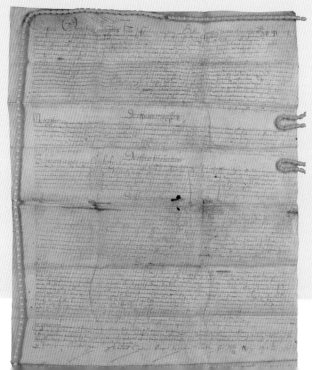

1600s

1611 *King James Bible* published, Dr Adrian Saravia is one of the translators

1613 Death of Adrian Saravia at Canterbury, 15 January

1629 The Cimitière des Frères, part of College estate but appropriated by Thomas Blanche as a private garden, is used for burial of plague victims

1633 Assistant master appointed to teach Reading, Writing, Music and Arithmetic – hitherto only Classics taught officially

1635 Foundation of three Oxford scholarships by Charles I

1678 Foundation of five scholarships by Bishop Morley at Pembroke, Oxford

1700s

1760 New school house built at a cost of £600 – later the Ozanne Building; English instead of French becomes the language of scholars

1789 Headmaster, Nicholas Carey, admits the school is 'languid'

1799 No scholars on roll

Map of St Pierre Port, 1787.

The Adventures of Messrs Snip, Green and Grumble,
from *The College Times*, 1853.

1800s

1800-5 Eighteen scholars on roll

1815 Only one scholar, James Amiraux Jérémie, later Regius Professor of Divinity, Cambridge

1816 No scholars on roll

1824 Sir John Colborne's enquiry into widespread mismanagement leads to re-chartering; the Revd Charles Stocker appointed Principal

1826 Colourful ceremony on 19 October heralds laying of new building foundation stone

1829 New building opened on 20 August; Bailiff asked that the occasion should be observed as an anniversary and kept as a holiday; the Revd George Proctor appointed Principal

1832 Eleazar Le Marchant Library bequest; the Revd William Davies appointed Principal

1847 Lt Governor Napier in dispute with Directors – Home Secretary appoints Dr Lushington special Visitor; the Revd John Bromby becomes Principal

1852 New College statutes approved by Queen Victoria, later confirmed by States; lock-ups created for boys 'too old to be caned'

1853 Bishop of Winchester made Permanent Visitor

1854 The Revd Arthur Corfe becomes Principal

1855 Principal's apartments lit by gas

1857 First College Sports at L'Ancresse Common; Directors plan 'open air' gymnasium

1861 Appointment of a drill instructor 'to be paid for by the boys'

1862 College Hall enlarged, stained-glass window placed in bay

1863 Tercentenary service held in Town Church and Grand Dinner hosted by OEs in the College Hall

1865 Gas lighting in boys' dormitories

1867 Directors in dispute with Principal and refuse to attend Speech Day

1868 School library established; the Revd John Oates becomes Principal

1870 Gas lights installed in Hall; first *Elizabethan* published

1872 Ladies' College founded by Sir Godfrey Carey (705), Bailiff

1877 Publication of *Consule Planco* (*The Good Old Days*) by Amias Andros (878)

1882 OEs begin purchase of fields at Rue à L'Or/King's Road

1888 The Revd William Penney appointed Principal and remains for 36 years; new cricket ground opened

1889 *The Elizabethan* reappears, published ever since; first inter-insular rugby football match with Victoria College, Jersey

1891 First pavilion constructed

1892 Purchase of College Field completed; OEA holds inaugural annual dinner; first Commemoration Service; 'Awkward Squad' (Squad) drill replaces some detentions

1896 *Fuimus, Sumus, Erimus* adopted as the OEA motto

1898 Debt on College Field cleared by OEA

1898 *College Register*, Vol I, published

1899 Telephone installed, telegraph pole erected in the playground

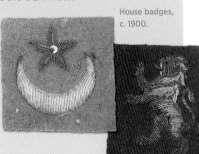

House badges, c. 1900.

1900s

1900 College orchestra formed with 11 instrumentalists

1901 Rugby football abandoned in favour of Association football

1902 Foundation of the OTC, later JTC and CCF

1903 Bicycle track at College Field removed to allow football pitches

1906 College VIII's first appearance in the Ashburton Shield at Bisley

1911 Sir Michael Sadler says College is indispensable to Guernsey's welfare

1918 College funding decided by new (States) Central Education Committee

Shooting medal, 1911.　　　　Woodwork class, 1920s.

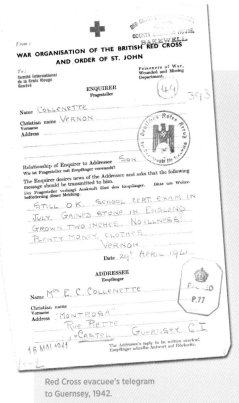

Red Cross evacuee's telegram to Guernsey, 1942.

Bicycles at College entrance, 1955.

1919 English Teachers' Superannuation Act and Burnham Scale of salaries introduced

1921 Royal visit of George V, Queen Mary and Princess Mary

1924 Dr Francis Hardy becomes Principal

1927 New gym opened by Bailiff, Sir Havilland de Sausmarez (1775)

1931 *College Register*, Vol II, published

1934 Reconstructed College organ rededicated by Bishop of Winchester

1935 Visit of Prince of Wales

1937 Hall Gallery built

1938 Main entrance through Porter's Lodge closed and a safer entrance built

1939 The Revd (William) Henry Milnes appointed Principal

1940 Evacuation of Elizabeth College to Derbyshire on 20 June

1945 Return of College to Guernsey on 1 August

1948 Lower School leaves main College site and housed at Saumarez Park

1949 Beechwood opens as new Lower School in Queen's Road

1950 Grange Club purchased and opened as a library/sixth form block

1951 *College Register*, Vol III, published

1952 Memorial Field opened

1955 Channel Islands receive first BBC TV transmissions

1956 Acquisition by States of land bordering Rue des Frères

Blazer badge, post-World War II.

CCF marches past FM Montgomery of Alamein, 1960.

Upland Road language lab, 1970s.

1957 The Queen and Prince Philip visit the College; John Day appointed Principal

1959 Gibson Fleming scholarships established

1959 Milnes Laboratories opened

1963 Quatercentenary visit by Queen Elizabeth the Queen Mother

1968 Swimming Pool Appeal

1972 Richard Wheadon appointed Principal

1974 OEs purchase a further 4.5 vergees of land adjacent to Memorial Field

1983 Expansion of Beechwood

1985 Re-instatement of College Assemblies in the newly refurbished St James

1988 John Doulton appointed Principal

1989 Shooting VIII wins Ashburton Shield

1990 Hockey pitch opened at the Memorial Field

1993 Sports hall opened, conversion of former gymnasium into teaching rooms

1995 German bunker demolished and College Hall entrance restored

1996 Acorn House pre-prep and pre-school opens

1997 Art block opened

1999 David Toze appointed Principal

2000s

2000 *College Register,* Vol IV, published

2001 Dr Nick Argent appointed Principal

2007 Establishment of Elizabeth College Foundation; fencing team wins Bartlett Cup for UK best boys' team

2008 Sixth form centre opened

2009 George Hartley appointed Principal

2010 Robin Roussel Pavilion opened at Memorial Field; college blazer badges re-instituted

2011 *History of Elizabeth College* published

2013 Celebrations for 450th anniversary

AUTHOR'S ACKNOWLEDGEMENTS, PICTURE CREDITS AND BIBLIOGRAPHY

I am extremely grateful to all those whose named contributions and comments already appear in the text and also for invaluable help from the following: Dr Darryl Ogier, States Archivist (see Author's Preface); John Fitzgerald (6372), a parent and friend of the College who has spent countless hours photographing College life; Sir Geoffrey Rowland (5603); Richard Hocart (5616); Richard Heaume (5043); Di Digard, John O'Neill and others at the Guernsey Press; Amanda Bennett and Ricky Allen of the Priaulx Library; Alan Howell and Helen Conlon of Guernsey Museums & Galleries; Stephen Foote (7003) of the Guernsey Society; La Société Guernesiaise; Odile Blanchette of Hauteville House, Lauren Williams; Sarah Miller; Major Evan Ozanne (4955); Tim Searle (6870); Nick Thomas (4211); Dr Peter Cogman (4812); Alex Rose (4704); all the staff and students at Elizabeth College who gave their time to provide information; the Rebsteins of St Martin's, for their hospitality on my frequent overnight visits to the island; many OEs and others who, only for reasons of space, are not on this list.

BRUCE PARKER

PICTURE CREDITS

Most of the images come from the Elizabeth College archives. The Publishers would like to thank Dot Carruthers for her invaluable help and expertise in sourcing and providing images.

The College and the Publishers would also like to thank the following people and organisations for allowing us to reproduce images:

pp4 and 7 John Fitzgerald; pp10/11 the Marquess of Salisbury; p12 (top) Guernsey Millennium Tapestry www.guernseytapestry.org.gg; p14 (top) Northamptonshire Record Office (below) the Marquess of Salisbury (right) © 2011 Guernsey Museums & Galleries, States of Guernsey (GMAG); p15 (top) John Fitzgerald (below) © World History Archive/TopFoto; pp16/17 © National Maritime Museum, Greenwich, London; p18 (right) © TopFoto/The Granger Collection; pp20/21 Roger Perrot; p22 (below) © GMAG; p23 (right) Island Archives, Guernsey; p24 (left) © 2011 GMAG; p25 (left) © The Priaulx Library, Guernsey (right) Dr Peter Harris; p26 Guernsey Greffe; p28 (top) Alan le Boutillier (top inset) © GMAG; p29 (bottom) © 2011 GMAG; p30 The Royal Court, States of Guernsey; p32 (top left) Barry Owen Jones (bottom right) © World History Archive/TopFoto; p33 (left) Guernsey Post Ltd (top right) © The Priaulx Library (bottom right) © 2011 GMAG; p35 (left) © TophamPicturepoint/TopFoto.co.uk (middle) © Brady-Handy Photograph Collection (Library of Congress); p36 © 2011 GMAG; p39 Courtesy of The Guernsey Press Co Ltd; p40 (top) © 2011 GMAG (bottom) Lord de Saumarez (right) Terry Wright; p41 (top) The Revd Peter Blee, Berwick Church, East Sussex (bottom) © 2011 GMAG; p42 (top) © The Priaulx Library, Guernsey; p42/3 Rick Le Page, p43 (bottom right) © 2011 GMAG; p45 © The Priaulx Library; pp46/7 © 2011 GMAG; p48 © 2011 GMAG; p50 © 2011 GMAG; p51 (top right) © Print Collector; p53 © The Priaulx Library; pp54/55 The Royal Collection © 2011 Her Majesty Queen Elizabeth II; p56 © National Portrait Gallery, London; p57 © 2011 GMAG; p58 Courtesy of The Guernsey Press Co Ltd; p59 (right) © Alexander Turnbull Library, Wellington, NZ; p60 (bottom right) Courtesy of The Guernsey Press Co Ltd; p61 (middle) Mrs Julia Halls; p62 (top) John Fitzgerald; p68 (both left) The Queens College Oxford (right) The Royal Court, States of Guernsey; p70 (left) © Bridgeman, National Army Museum London

(right) Royal Army Medical Corps; p71 (top left) Royal
Marines Museum, Southsea (right) Guernsey Post Ltd
(bottom right) Royal Hampshire Regiment Trust; pp72/73
and p74 (left) VisitGuernsey; p75 (top middle) © The
National Portrait Gallery, London (below left) Guernsey
Post Ltd; p76 © 2011 GMAG; p77 (left) © 2011 GMAG
(right) © The Illustrated London News Ltd/Mary Evans;
p78 Wodehouse archive; p79 (top) © The Priaulx Library,
Guernsey; p83 (right) Courtesy of The Guernsey Press Co
Ltd (bottom) © The Priaulx Library, Guernsey; p85 (top
right) Courtesy of The Guernsey Press Co Ltd (middle)
Guernsey Post Ltd; p86 (top) John Fitzgerald; p87 (top)
© The Priaulx Library, Guernsey; p89 (top right) Rick Le
Page (inset) © 2011 GMAG; p90 (bottom) Rick Le Page
(right) John Fitzgerald; p91 (left) © Bridgeman, Private
Collection; p92 (left) The Potting Shed; p96 (top left)
© 2011 GMAG; pp100/101 © The Priaulx Library,
Guernsey; p103 (top) John Davis (bottom) JA Ideler;
p104 (right) Oldham Evening Chronicle, p105 (top)
© Pictorial Press Ltd/Alamy; p106/7 (behind) © TopFoto/
Granger Collection; p107 (bottom) Oldham Evening
Chronicle; p108 (bottom left) Thelma Collenette;
p112 (top) © The Priaulx Library, Guernsey (inset)
Guernsey Post Office Ltd; p114 (left) Rob Champion;
p115 (top right) © 2011 GMAG; p121 (top) John Fitzgerald;
p122 (left) © Priaulx Library, Guernsey; p124/5 John
Fitzgerald; p126 (left) and p128 (bottom) Courtesy of The
Guernsey Press Co Ltd; p129 (top and left) John Fitzgerald
(bottom right) By permission of the States of Guernsey,
Treasury and Resources; pp132/3 John Fitzgerald;
p140/1 (bottom) Pierre Bisson; p143, pp144/5, p146 (top
right and bottom left) John Fitzgerald; p147 (right) The
Potting Shed; p148 (bottom left) Courtesy of The Guernsey
Press Co Ltd; p150 John Fitzgerald; p151 (bottom left)
Northamptonshire Records Office (right) Island Archives,
Guernsey; p153 (top) Rick Le Page.

BIBLIOGRAPHY

A Headmaster Remembers, F Hardy
An Island Assembly, R Hocart
Annals of British Norman Isles, J Jacob
Calendar of State Papers, National Archives
Causeries Guernesiases, P Stapfer
Diary of the Occupation of Guernsey, JC Sauvary
Directors' Minute Books, Elizabeth College
Elizabeth College, 1563–1963, VG Collenette
Elizabeth College in Exile, VG Collenette
Elizabeth College Registers, Vols I, II, III & IV
Elizabeth College Enquiry, 1824
History of Guernsey, W Berry
History of Guernsey, J Duncan
History of Guernsey, FB Tupper
Kennedy of Cape York, E Beale
Napier, HA Bruce
Notes on a Cellar Book, G Saintsbury
PG Wodehouse portrait of a Master, D Jasen
Queen Victoria's journal, edited by A Helps
Recollections of a Sussex Parson (1912), EB Ellman
Reformation in Guernsey, DM Ogier
Robert, S Morley
'Scrap Books', G Saintsbury
The Channel Islands, HD Inglis
The Channel Islands Under Tudor Government, AJ Eagleston
The Commando Who Came Home to Spy, W Bell
The Elizabethan
The Making of New Zealand Cricket, G Ryan
The RAF—A Personal experience, P Le Cheminant
Transactions of La Société Guernesiase
Victor Hugo, G Robb
Victor Hugo à Guernesey, P Stapfer

INDEX